CONTEMPORARY PLAYWRIGHTS
ROBERT BOLT

CONTEMPORARY PLAYWRIGHTS

ROBERT BOLT
BY
RONALD HAYMAN

HEINEMANN · LONDON

Heinemann Educational Books Ltd
London Edinburgh Melbourne Toronto
Singapore Auckland Johannesburg
Ibadan Hong Kong Nairobi

SBN 435 18430 X (cased edition)
SBN 435 18405 9 (paperback)

© Ronald Hayman 1969
First published in paperback 1969
First published as a cased edition 1970

Published by Heinemann Educational Books Ltd
48 Charles Street, London W1X 8AH
Printed in Great Britain by
Cox & Wyman Ltd, London, Fakenham and Reading

CONTENTS

ACKNOWLEDGEMENTS

The photographs of *Flowering Cherry*, *Gentle Jack* and *A Man for All Seasons* are reproduced by courtesy of Angus McBean Ltd, and that of *The Thwarting of Baron Bolligrew* by courtesy of Dominic.

ROBERT BOLT

Texts

THREE PLAYS:
Flowering Cherry
A Man for All Seasons
The Tiger and the Horse

Gentle Jack
The Thwarting of Baron Bolligrew

These are all published by Heinemann Educational Books, who also publish *The Tiger and the Horse* and *A Man for All Seasons* in the Hereford Series with introductions by E. R. Wood
Gentle Jack is also available in French's Acting Edition

Performances

1st April 1957	*The Critic and the Heart* at Oxford Playhouse, directed by Jack Minster
21st November 1957	*Flowering Cherry* at the Haymarket, directed by Frith Banbury with Sir Ralph Richardson and Celia Johnson
1st July 1960	*A Man for All Seasons* at the Globe, directed by Noel Willman with Paul Scofield and Leo McKern
24th August 1960	*The Tiger and the Horse* at the Queen's, directed by Frith Banbury with Sir Michael Redgrave and Vanessa Redgrave

Robert Bolt

28th November 1963	*Gentle Jack* at the Queen's, directed by Noel Willman with Dame Edith Evans and Kenneth Williams
11th December 1965	*The Thwarting of Baron Bolligrew* at the Aldwych, directed by Trevor Nunn with Leo McKern

Films

Lawrence of Arabia

Doctor Zhivago

A Man for All Seasons

PREFACE

This book is divided into three parts:
1. an interview with Robert Bolt which is mainly biographical;
2. a critique of the six plays;
3. an interview about the critique, taking each chapter separately.
The reader therefore has the alternative of reading the book straight through or stopping at the end of each chapter to read the discussion I had about it with Robert Bolt. Readers who want to consult the book on one particular play will find that the list of contents gives page references both for my chapter on it and for the section of the interview about that chapter.

I should like to say how grateful I am to Robert Bolt for taking time to work with me in this way, and it would be as well to explain why I wanted to adopt this method of approach.

There is enormous scope for variation in the relationship that subsists between a playwright, his life and his plays. From the plays of Beckett, Pinter or Whiting, you get to know only a little about the man and next to nothing about his life. From Osborne's plays, especially the early ones, you learn a lot about the man and a little about his life. From Strindberg's plays, you get a great deal of both the man and his life, for there's comparatively little filtering in the way he projects himself and his experience into them. The same is true of D. H. Lawrence's plays.

With Bolt, there is an unusual and very interesting relationship between the man, the life and the plays. The life has been an extraordinarily eventful one. As a child he stole and came bottom of the class. As an army officer he was still a member of the Communist Party. And as a film writer, he served a prison sentence in the middle of working on *Lawrence of Arabia* because of having been a member of the Committee of a Hundred and refusing to be bound over. Although he's never projected himself at all directly into any of his characters or drawn directly on his own experience, he's always written out of urgent and very strong feelings, and the preoccupations behind his plays and behind his life are recognizably the same, which

Robert Bolt

may be one of the reasons why the things he puts into his plays aren't always quite the same things as an audience gets out of them. Even the most sympathetic critic couldn't come away from either a performance or a reading of *Gentle Jack* – or even a much more straightforward play like *Flowering Cherry* or *The Tiger and the Horse* – with a clear grasp on all the points Robert Bolt makes about these plays in our discussion. The fact that he's still changing his style so much from one play to another may be a sign that he's looking for a form in which everything he puts into a play will come out exactly as he intends it. But many of the points that fail to come out of these first six plays are good and important points, and I was very glad indeed that they came out in the interview.

FIRST INTERVIEW

RONALD HAYMAN: *You were born in 1924 and it says in one of the biographical notes I've read that you were the son of a small shopkeeper – which makes me picture a little man in a little shop.*

ROBERT BOLT: He was both I think – a small man, and the keeper of a small shop. It sold furniture and glass and china. It was new furniture later, but earlier there was second-hand furniture. Throughout my childhood, yes, this shop – and the sound of the shop bell, and the entrance, and the three steps down to the shop from the house – these are very specific memories.

Later you seemed to be glad to get away from Manchester. Can you say anything in general about your childhood? Was it a happy childhood?

Well it's strange: I don't see why it shouldn't have been but it wasn't: I wouldn't be a child again for anything. I know, looking back, that the whole colour of my life as a child was a very dark one – very gloomy, fraught, self-doubting, self-contemptuous, lots of petty delinquency, very bad behaviour at school, cordially disliked by my teachers – I think with good reason – a terrible worry to my parents – a real nightmare to them I think. I used to steal things from shops, and get into fights, and was secretive and violent. I was at the bottom of the class, not just from time to time but *all* the time and with really the kind of reports that a parent doesn't just laugh off but thinks 'My God, what's going to happen to the boy?' – which I know my parents did, and so did I. But although I was so unhappy at school I dreaded the day of leaving school because I was quite certain I wouldn't be able to cope at all. The idea of having to be a grown-up, and to look after myself was horrifying to me. Although the kind of show I was putting up was one of great independence and rebellion, in point of fact – like most rebellious children – I was very much a child, I think.

And what all this was about I simply don't know. My parents were a little bit strict perhaps, but not outrageously strict; they had genuinely high standards, and certainly they were very loving and concerned parents. My elder brother was very successful at school,

1

Robert Bolt

which is a classic reason for a younger brother to be a bit of a failure, but I can't see why it should have had this really, I think, quite damaging effect on me. Very odd, isn't it?

I can remember three distinct phases. When I was about seven, the whole business of school seemed laughably easy – I couldn't believe that this was all there was to it and I was more or less effortlessly the top of the class or near, the bright little boy, you see, until I was seven. Then quite suddenly in one year – this was the year when I left the little preparatory school – I began to be a bad boy and won a reputation for being a bad boy, and that went on from bad to worse until round the age of about fourteen or fifteen. I was quite seriously naughty and might have got into some serious trouble if I hadn't been so lucky.

But what happened when you were seven?

I can just remember this particular year and I think some kind of conceit – I was younger than the other boys in the class and yet was still the top of the class and I can remember my father telling me that I had a sort of knack for knowing what people wanted and giving it to them – in the way of personality and things to say – that half used to take his breath away and half to frighten him, because it was ghoulish, he said, to see a little boy manipulating adults. So I evidently either enjoyed or had a great need of approval or attention, and maybe at the age of seven I decided that it was a more spectacular, easier way to get it to be naughty than to be good – I don't know – but I can remember, it was a very violent and radical change. And I can remember a grim, long drawn-out declension into – oh, self-contempt really sums it up, and violence. I was a terrible show-off, a terrible liar and so on, but you know, that's no contradiction. And then I can remember my first experiment in being a good boy again, and I remember one occasion in particular in school and a terrible wave of anger at the end of an English lesson – I was always very good at English – when I say very good at it I don't mean the grammar and the spelling but you know, reading bits of poetry and stories and then discussing them – I'd always got lots to say and could always interest not only the teacher but the class – this was very easy meat for me you see – I can remember this early experiment in being a good boy, at the end of the class, the teacher saying something very complimentary to me, like, 'This is the way you should carry on all the time, and then you'd see what a splendid chap you'd be, the life and soul of the party and so on' – and then this anger – I almost wanted to cry because I felt the whole thing had been false and that he ought to know that it was false and that if this was all that being good added up to, then it wasn't worth it. You know, a kind of precociously existential position overtook me for half an hour or so – I can remember anger and a terrible sense of loss, because I thought, 'My goodness, perhaps this is really all these good people are – they're just sort of putting up this ridiculous pretence.' And I suppose to some extent this is still my state of mind – I think these childhood preoccupations have never quite left me.

But when did the major turn of the tide come about enjoying yourself?

Well, I don't know. I've never been awfully good at enjoying myself. You see, come to think of it, it takes a puritan – doesn't it ? – to make a duty out of enjoying yourself. Which is Lawrence's message. Blood and Sex and the Natural Impulses are Very Enjoyable and therefore you had better damn well Enjoy them or you're for the stick! Your old classical writers, or even your orthodox Romantic writers took it for granted that sex was fun and said, 'Now what are we going to do about this?' But Lawrence discovered it like – like vegetarianism. My attitude to enjoyment has always been a little bit like that. In the first place I'm always really more easy in my mind if there's a good moral reason for enjoyment – for example for going on holiday. It's nice if it's going to improve my health if I've been working hard so that I ought to relax so that I can do some more work better. That's the first line of defence against enjoyment. And then the second thing of course is this Lawrencian one that enjoying yourself is good and legitimate and you ought to be able to. Enjoying myself is something I really have to work at.

But I mean just enjoying what goes on. You give the impression of liking people and liking life and liking what's happening around you.

I do find almost everything indiscriminately interesting. I'm not quite sure whether I do *like* things. I suppose I do – yes, because I don't have a scientist's analytical interest in things; I do find the whole phenomenon and experience of living exciting, I suppose – which is a definition of liking it, isn't it? But it seems to me that I so to

3

Robert Bolt

speak owe God an apology for not enjoying myself more, considering what good fortune I've had in various respects. I find it very difficult just to accept the situation and go with the stream without worrying about it; I am usually trying to get beyond it, trying to make it safe.

But I think I know when I began to enjoy life, if that is what I am doing. You see, at the end of my school career I ended up in a very pleasant form called Remove Beta, which is a kind of sump or appendix at the bottom of Manchester Grammar School for draining off ineducable material. And I had a couple of leisurely years taking School Certificate. I took it twice and did rather worse the second time, having simply deteriorated. And my father said, 'Look, you've made your bed, you must lie on it.' I was at panic stations – I didn't know what to do and drifted into an insurance office where I was a sort of office boy, running messages, looking after the boilers and so on. And such small clerical duties as I had to perform I did very badly. I think this is the origin of Jim Cherry in *Flowering Cherry*. Again there was an overwhelming sense – a double sense of being too good for it, and at the same time an awareness that I wasn't good enough, because I wasn't as efficient as the other people. My head was full of rarefied nonsense but I couldn't remember to post letters at the right time with the right stamps on them. And this was the first time I ever consciously and in set terms hated anything – I hated the office, I *really* hated it – I hated the life and was determined not to go on.

Well of course the war had started and I was going to be called up at the end of a couple of years anyway so this put a deadline to it. But at the end of one year I met a teacher, not my own, but one of my brother's teachers in Manchester who asked me how I was liking it and I told him I was hating it. He said he thought this was very good and the first positive reaction he could remember me having to anything. And he said, 'Look, if I could wangle some sort of university entry for you, would you take it?' And I said, 'Try me.'

There was a war-time entry for a degree in commerce. I didn't want a degree in commerce. I didn't want anything; I just did not want to go to the office any more. It was prevarication, a year's reprieve. I had to take three subjects at Advanced Level, which I did by studying in the evenings just for five weeks. And that was extraordinary, you see, because I covered a year's syllabus in the evenings without a teacher in five weeks, simply because I desperately wanted to. This is something which as a teacher I never forgot – if you can arouse a child's desire to learn, you are not half-way home, you're four-fifths of the way home. There are two ways of arousing his desire: there is a bad way – fear – which is really what aroused my desire. Or of course, ideally, by making the child see that the subject's interesting and worth pursuing and is applicable and has something to do with its own life.

Do you think that has any bearing on the ways you use of arousing audience curiosity?

Yes, I hate the idea of an audience sitting down and thinking, 'Well this is really rather dull stuff but Bolt's an awfully nice chap and he usually has something interesting to say so we'd better apply ourselves.' They have paid money to have their desire aroused and I think the great weapon is, as you have just implied, the desire of the audience to know about the characters on stage. Just a straightforward, childlike, primitive desire to be told. This does imply all the tricks, old and new, for arousing their curiosity. For me certainly the essential thing is that the audience should want to know – not want to know what happens next but want to know about these characters, about what they're up to, about what can be abstracted from the pattern of events. They should *not* be sitting there applying themselves with conscious effort. And this is certainly true of children. Desire is everything, if anything is to be learned.

So for you – going back to your life – this was the first year in which you were really using your mind and enjoying using it?

That's right. A tremendous relief to realize that I could, because despite all the evidence to the contrary I'd remained convinced that I was a highly intelligent person, though I was unique in this opinion. And then of course the first year at university was really the opening of the gates of paradise for me. Absolutely marvellous. I was more or less drunk the whole year on freedom and ideas and new friends and oh everything. Girls – the first time I'd ever been with girls, you see, really. I had no sisters. Everything was just suddenly marvellous.

You just had one brother?

Just the one brother, yes, and boys' schools, you see. They let me into an Honours school at the University instead of the commerce school and I did well at the end of the year so they let me back after the war for another three years. I took History. But that first year was the first time I can remember consciously thinking that life was good.

I was a Marxist then and a Communist and of course economics was all that mattered – economics governed history, history governed politics and politics was life and therefore economics was life and so economic history was all that really mattered.

You joined the Party?

Oh yes. I was very enthusiastic – eighteen when I joined and I stayed a member for five years including three years in the forces, where theoretically you weren't supposed to be a member but you were and there was always a Party cell in every camp. And then again when I was demobilized, it took me about eighteen months to realize that I was so hostile to so many things in the Party that the only sensible thing was to get out. A very difficult thing to do of course, to leave the Party . . . you feel like a crab without a shell.

It's interesting though that as you've formulated it, it was hostility to what was going on inside the Party that made you come out and presumably hostility to what was going on in society that made you go in.

Oh, quite true, I'm afraid, yes. Certainly I joined the Party largely out of dissatisfactions – that is, with what I felt was wrong. At the same time I would have expressed these with the accompanying view of what I thought the Party was going to do to put it all right. I believed passionately that Russia was a better society than ours. Then when I left the Party that was almost entirely negative too in as much as I didn't leave the Party thinking, 'Oh well, capitalism's not so bad after all.' I thought and still think that capitalism is bad, so that I had no positive. But the day to day being-in-the-Party was terribly on my nerves – the chivvying and more and more finding myself in a minority at Party meetings. They had no doubt at all that the Poles were simply overjoyed to be swallowed up in the Soviet Union. It was ridiculous to have been a member of the Communist Party for four years as I had then and not to have realized that it has nothing to do with democracy or freedom. It's a self-justifying organization. The essence of Humanity is Progress. The Proletariat is the Progressive Class. The Communist Party is the Party of the Proletariat. So what's good for the Party is good for humanity. It's a fatal frame of mind.

But when you're inside it you can't see it in that way?

You see it and accept it. If you say to a Communist 'But why is it good for humanity because it is good for the Party?' it's rather like asking a Christian, 'Why should I do what God wants?'

This must have been a major swing in your whole way of thinking about everything when you came out.

It was. When I left the Party, typically enough you see, I was looking around for another absolute. I still hadn't got the message, which I take it is that you've more or less got to take life as it comes. That you can have a man who is a good marksman and another man who's a bad marksman and another man who is a moderate marksman and you can arrange these three in a line of competence, as it were, in a graph, but because of that it doesn't mean to say that there is somewhere some *absolutely* perfect marksman at the end of the graph. This is a very simple proposition but it took me the first thirty years of my life to realize it. When you state it, it seems so obvious that one wonders why it needs stating, but anyway I suppose because we're brought up in a Christian civilization one works the other way round. You are told of some metaphysical ideal goodness to which you must approximate. However, when I left the Party, I flirted with people like Martin Buber, the Jewish mystic, and Zen and Lao-Tse-Taoism and a little bit with the Christian mystics. Buber had an effect on the way I thought and therefore a faint effect on the way I lived and felt. What I was trying to say in the preface to *A Man for all Seasons* was not just that it's the individual that counts but that the individual is all there *is*. For better or worse we are born individually, the unit of consciousness is the individual and whatever there is for good or bad comes in these penny packets. There's no way of uniting two of these penny packets together except possibly in the moment of love. It is not just a matter of saying that the community's a comparative abstraction which is usually an excuse for individualism in the capitalist sense of people being nasty to one another. Philosophically and spiritually you are stuck with yourself and any good you achieve you will achieve in yourself and any evil you suffer you will suffer in yourself.

Robert Bolt

I do find it hard to reconcile that with what you've said about wanting to resemble Brecht more than any other playwright.

Well, on aesthetic grounds. I love the chunky classical four-square quality of Brecht. The whole thing about a work of art is that it is an object – it either works on its own or it doesn't. I hate it if the artist is so to speak leaning on me, warmly breathing his own emotion over me. All the emotion must be trapped and captured and used technically in the work. This is my aim. I find it very difficult to be gentle about the emotions, just to let them run. I can deal with emotions at crisis pitch but I seem to find it very difficult simply to accept them as the ordinary run of the stuff of life. Thought seems in my plays to be the normal run of stuff and emotion is only called on in moments of crisis. I think this is a weakness and I don't think this is true of life. In fact I think the whole split between thought and emotion is a nonsensical one.

Coming back to these three phases, how did the intermediate one shade off into the third?

Very gradually and in the process of writing, really. I was always writing something, never finishing anything. As a child I wrote.

Did you?

Oh yes, in the lavatory. Exercise books full of stuff. And read, fantastically. Dreamed, read, mooned about the library. Walter Scott ... And I used to write terrible historical novels – quasi-pornographic, with long torture scenes, from the age of about nine onwards. And then when I was a student, I was always writing terribly strange high-flown essays full of references I really had no right to make because I didn't really know the works I was referring to. And then when I became a teacher there was this nativity play I had to write.

When you knew after writing just six lines of dialogue that this was the thing you wanted to do with your life.

That was an astonishing turning point, very conscious. I've had two or three of those in my life and I can remember very vividly a sense of almost physically, turning a corner. And also knowing that this was in some sense the last corner. That this was what I was going to do and that I was going to succeed or fail by this.

Let's catch up, could we, on the story of your life up to the point where you were teaching in Exeter.

Well I was a year at the University and joined the Party, after the office – this was 1942 I suppose, yes. Oh, yes, yes, yes, I was very fond of music when I was at the office. The great outlet was storms of romantic music – Beethoven, Schubert, Wagner and what little money I had I spent on records. But more of this at university, you see, much more music and the Party and the revolution and the war and then the year I was called up and going into the RAF and oh everything just larger than life and more vivid. A terrific year. Then the RAF and again a great expansion because you see I went to Manchester University, so fundamentally I hadn't left home.

You were living at home still?

Partly at home, partly in digs but very much under the wing of home. But my parents again extraordinarily tolerant and broadminded – didn't mind if I stayed out all night. They were delighted because it was the first time that (a) I'd ever done any work and (b) it was the first time they'd seen me happy. They were loving, concerned parents and they must have known that something was violently wrong with me. As well as disapproving they must have felt very sorry for me. And they were happy about this transformation that took place in this year. You know – just suddenly having time for other people because I was no longer absolutely racked by my own difficulties. Being able to be cheerful and polite and moderately kind with people. It must have been a relief for them.

And for you.

Oh, unspeakable. And then in the army to London, I think almost the first time I'd ever been to London. Aircrew Reception Centre – a lot of public schoolboys who struck me as being enormously charming, of whom of course I disapproved on principle but some of whom I liked enormously as individuals because they were so witty and their manners were so nice and so on. Some of them I hated because they were snobbish. Then, let me see, oh, lots of hanging about. It was at a time when we were having very heavy losses and they'd over-recruited for aircrew, thinking that they were going to get mown down. So there was about a year of doing absolutely nothing. I went out to South Africa to continue the training – another marvellous experience. That was the first time I'd ever been abroad. Going abroad on a ship was a tremendous excitement. Blue sea and flying fish and so on – realizing that all these things did exist outside books.

And then in South Africa I developed airsickness and looking back on it I'm not sure that this wasn't cowardice. Because I was good at it, at the elementary stages of flying. I was picked to be a pilot rather than a navigator. Anyway I was too sick to be any further use to them.

So I went into the army and got a commission and that again was interesting. I went to Sandhurst and again I was partly repelled and partly seduced by it. Reluctantly I had to admit that there was a great deal of glamour and beauty in this upper class assumption, you see. All of which was helping to undermine I suppose the emotional basis of my Communism, because as a Communist it was not merely that the workers were right and the bosses were wrong, but that the workers were morally and aesthetically beautiful. Working-class art was good, football matches were good. Ascot was not merely overprivileged, it was ugly and pretentious. And to realize that Ascot might be charming and beautiful, and to be unable quite to stencil this out from my own perception rocked the boat. But I would claim that I have always had some loyalty to observable fact.

Then I went to West Africa – the Gold Coast, this time. Incidentally the Cape in South Africa when I was aircrew, waiting for the boat back, was absolutely marvellous. Met John Cranko and theatre people and artists – they made a great fuss of the RAF. Wonderful, oh, wine and peaches and all kinds of harmless junketings and again girls at parties. The whole thing was madly glamorous to me and again eroding this northern, nonconformist, completely moral and in any case Marxist view of right and wrong. It was beginning to dawn on me that life could be pleasurable without doing any harm to anybody.

I hated being an officer a good deal. I hated the mess. I'd hated the awful discomforts of barrack life, as a private. Bad food, chivvying, needless bullying by sergeants, but there was a kind of something respectable about being in the ranks whereas being a young officer in a non-combatant unit at that stage of the war was really very humiliating. Comforts were extreme but most of my fellow officers seemed to me shabby and their preconceptions nasty. They were real fodder to my Marxism. Most of them were everything I thought a decadent upper class should be – silly, irresponsible, not even good officers. I was just over three years in the forces – then back to Manchester, still as a party member.

Were you writing anything in these three years?

Yes, little bits – essays, poems, beginnings of stories. It wasn't until I started writing plays that I hit my stride.

You never happened on that dialogue form?

No. It had always seemed to me bewilderingly difficult, also I'd hardly ever seen a play. I don't suppose I'd seen more than half a dozen plays in my life when I wrote the first one. I'd always had the ancient Puritan feeling that Theatre was sinful – not in my case sexually sinful, which I think it probably was for my parents, and I may have picked up a bit of that attitude. But to me it was just flighty and also impossibly glamorous and bohemian. Perhaps I was too attracted to know how attracted I was.

What about the other two turning points in your life?

When I came back from South Africa, the last place I'd been was Capetown. To my mind it's more beautiful than anything I've seen in the Mediterranean – and of course an exceedingly privileged life if your skin is the right colour. And I'd had my first really serious affair with a girl, Well, a ten-day trip back on a very fast ship, the *Andes*, straight from their summer to our winter. Liverpool. Freezing cold. On to a train and home to Manchester for disembarkation leave. And I can remember grinding into Central Station in Manchester through those industrial slums and factories which I knew like the back of my hand, you see I'd never seen anything else. And looking out of the window, and like a physical blow in the chest – realizing that this was ugly. And I was astonished, and I thought, 'My goodness, this is what people mean by ugliness.' It had never dawned on me because I'd never seen anything else. I can remember for example being quite surprised – I don't know how old I was but not just a tiny tot – by the realization that trees were not naturally sooty; and this was the same sort of thing at a more mature level, a similar realization that life didn't have to be like this – just in terms of awful orange brick and black mill chimneys – but also in a much wider deeper sense

11

Robert Bolt

that life didn't have to be the way it always had been. It was something else I'd thought was a given quantity which turned out not to be. Either it could be altered or it could be escaped. One didn't have to stay in Manchester, and the moment I got my degree I was up and away, and I've never been back.

In writing for an audience I suppose you make concessions in the sense that what you finally get down on the page is a simplification of what you would ideally like to get down.

Not really, you know, because you hope that the play *form* will imply the complexity. Obviously the situation cannot be as complicated as the way we're talking now. You hope you have a simple situation but, as with Thomas More, so surrounded by emotional complexities that the full complexity of it will be adumbrated. But I see what you mean. You mean that in my plays I'm always taking as it were black and white situations and putting my characters on the spot and saying 'Now what are you going to do?'

But are you making concessions for a commercial audience?

Consciously, never. I would say that this is the nature of playwriting. If you don't want to write like this, if you don't enjoy doing this, if you feel that doing this for your audience gets in the way of what you're really trying to say, then you shouldn't be a playwright. I love it. It helps me to say what I want to say; it doesn't get in the way. If I am communicating something in the form of a play, I have to use different vocabulary for the various situations, conflicts, stances taken than I would if I were writing in the form of a lecture.

Fine, but if you are writing a play you have a certain audience in mind and something depends on the size of that audience, doesn't it?

Very good, very good. I do accept the given audience that is to say a largely middle-class, West End, theatre-going audience.

But in Gentle Jack *you were taking a big chance and a lot of them didn't see the point you were making.*

Sure, and this is my fault, I should have done it better.

But is it something that can be done?

I don't know. Who knows? You have to keep trying. I'm going to try again.

What about writing for films? Do you find youself simplifying for a bigger audience?

12

Yes, I think so. I think I do. And to what extent this is the nature of the beast, and to what extent it's that I always work – or have done hitherto – with a film director; I don't know. I think that if I were writing a film myself, I *might* be inclined to take a few more chances than I have done writing films so far with David Lean and Freddy Zinnemann. But I don't know; it's easier said than done. And I don't like the kind of film director who just chances his arm fashionably and hopes for the best.

Let's get back to your life. You started writing plays with this nativity play.

Yes, that was in 1950.

And then you wrote twelve radio plays while you were still teaching.

That's counting children's plays and most of those were only half an hour long. It was about half a dozen long ones and half a dozen short ones.

What was this about going to prison for nuclear disarmament activities?

That was another kind of crisis point for me. I am absolutely opposed to the possession and making of atomic weapons. People say, 'Well, you don't object to little bombs, why do you object to big bombs?' This is logical but it isn't common sense. I was talking to Bertrand Russell about this and he said, 'Yes, it's astonishing how people hate the intrusion of common sense into morality.' They hate it because if you allow that common sense has anything to do with morality then you may have to do something about morality whereas if you keep morality pure and rarefied, you're not called on to do anything. Anyway it seemed to me that the atomic bomb was something that one was more or less bound to dig in one's heels about, and I talked a lot about this and wrote a certain amount about it. And then I had this letter from Bertrand Russell saying he wanted this 'Committee of a Hundred' forming and that the idea was to make some token breach of the law and court imprisonment, because legitimate means seemed to be having no impression at all on the politicians. So I wrote back and said that I hated the idea of breaking the law, which I do, as you'll have gathered from *A Man for all Seasons* – I have respect for the law because I think that the human being is a potentially chaotic and destructive creature, and society and the law are infinitely valuable, but I said that I would be one of his hundred, so I was one of his

Robert Bolt

hundred, and to cut a long story short eventually I was put in prison with Russell and a few others. And this again was a turning point because, although I blush to confess it, I think that throughout my Communist and Marxist period, I had always really had the feeling that policemen were there to look after me, and would not do anything *really* nasty to a nice person like myself. And when I broke the law and the police put me in prison for it, I was deeply shocked. And there I was with rough warders and tin plates and a jerry in the cell. And then all hell broke loose because I was in the middle of writing *Lawrence* and they were shooting it as I wrote it, more or less, at that time, and the whole machine ground to a standstill. Sam Spiegel, who was the producer, just went absolutely mad – 'So have these people got to lose their jobs and lose thousands of dollars just so that you can go to heaven when you die?' was his line. He actually came down to the prison finally. So after a fortnight I bound myself over and came out, and bitterly and instantly regretted it. This was another big turning point because I felt that although there were very good reasons why I should, I knew that ultimately I should *not* have come out and it was simply because Sam had built up the pressure to such an extent that I couldn't hold out.

For about six months afterwards I found it very hard to look at myself in the mirror, because it seemed to me, however it was wrapped up, almost pure weakness. I gave the money away – that is the money I earned as a result of coming out of prison, gave it oddly enough to Arnold's Centre 42.

You said in some earlier interview that you didn't start writing until you knew how the play was going to end.

Yes, that is true. I think that is still true. Yes, I still need to know the end of the play – maybe not now so mechanically as I did. I need to know that this was the starting situation and this was its result and there has to be a maybe totally unconscious, inexplicable, maybe even ineffable link between the situation and its results. There has to be something inevitable. To me the ideal audience reaction is not, 'My goodness, I would never have expected that,' but 'Oh my God, of course.'

One thing that has struck me is that where most playwrights seem to have a hero who in a lot of ways is an idealized version of themselves, you write

*character parts. You don't put yourself straight into More or any of the
other heroes. There are no coefficients of yourself.*

Obviously one must be *all* one's characters ... No, no ... How
interesting, yes, I see, I'd never thought, yes, maybe, maybe, in fact,
you see this sort of gloom and darkness which I vaguely feel in my
childhood – maybe this kind of dispassion is some sort of escape. Maybe I still – it's only just dawned on me – but maybe I still dislike
myself sufficiently to be grateful for the opportunity to think
about somebody else.

*This is only a wild guess but I wonder whether the way to embody more
of the positives that you left out of* Gentle Jack *would be to think more
kindly of yourself and put yourself into the play.*

Yes, undoubtedly, yes, and maybe this is what's happening. I think
on the whole I'm liking writing more and I'm liking living more. I
suppose this means that I'm liking myself more or at least learning to
tolerate myself more. Mind you what I'd really love would be to feel
that the play *in its totality* was me, not this character or that.

*A lot of the things you've written suggest an identification with the
Christian point of view but you describe yourself as something between
an agnostic and an aetheist.*

I ought to be religious in the sense that I'm comfortable thinking in
religious terms and altogether I seem naturally constituted to be
religious. It just is my misfortune that I have no religion.

You weren't brought up in any?

Indeed I was, yes, I was brought up Methodist. I can remember my
father saying to me when I was complaining about having to go to
chapel – which I did twice every Sunday – he said, 'When you're old
enough, you can choose for yourself,' and I said, 'When will I be old
enough?' and he said, 'Oh, well, when you're sixteen.' So when I was
sixteen I said, 'Can I now choose for myself whether to go to chapel or
not?' and he said, 'Yes, you can,' and I've never been since. The
interesting thing is that neither has he.

But the fact remains that the groundswell of my thought only
makes sense on the assumption that there is Somebody to whom I am
responsible.

THE CRITIC AND THE HEART

The Critic and the Heart was produced in April 1957 at Oxford Playhouse. Robert Bolt has since said that he's unenthusiastic about the play because it's perfectly orthodox in style. What he did, knowing so little about theatre at the time, was to study Somerset Maugham's play *The Circle,* analysing its structure and then modelling his own play on it, even following the same act lengths. In substance and in dialogue, though, the play bears no resemblance to its model and Bolt quickly showed a strong talent for arousing an audience's interest and creating a clear dramatic confrontation.

He starts off with two characters *doing* something: Muriel comes out into the garden to help Winifred, who is struggling with a trestle table which has collapsed. Winifred is fifty-five and the stage direction describes her as 'one of society's, not one of Nature's spinsters'; Muriel is young and attractive but 'without the freakish gimmick necessary to turn heads'. When they've got the table up, they produce a home-made banner which proclaims 'Budmouth Society of Arts' and Winifred, like Gwendoline Dean at the beginning of *The Tiger and the Horse,* seems amiably but strikingly eccentric, so the scene has immediately aroused our curiosity both about the characters and about what their preparations are for.

When Dr Barret arrives and refuses to answer Muriel's question about the condition of Winifred's brother, the painter William Brazier, this makes us even more curious. Their dialogue skilfully plants the points that Muriel is going to have a baby and that the likeable doctor doesn't like William. He may be a genius but he is certainly an ego-maniac, and the doctor blames him for making Winifred into the neurotic mess she is today.

Bolt also shows a talent for creating a story with a lot of component pieces which slot into each other neatly and each of which provides a subject of dramatic conflict. The rash on Winifred's hands, for instance, obviously caused psycho-somatically, is a sort of thermometer for her condition as it gets worse or better. It soon causes a minor struggle with the doctor when she refuses to show him her hands, and a bigger one when we find out why. She's been waiting on William herself instead of letting Muriel do it and she's done nothing about getting a nurse to look after him, because he doesn't want one.

When Barret goes, the conversation establishes a neat parallel between the two women: Muriel is working to support her artist husband Pat, just as Winifred has sacrificed her legacy and her life to looking after her artist brother. A telephone call establishes that Newton Reeves, the well-known art critic, is expected on a visit, and when Potter, the local solicitor, arrives, the conversation pleasantly creates the atmosphere of the village fete they are preparing for.

> We shall skittle for a pig in the traditional manner – the gentlemen that is – a less rustic trophy will be found for the ladies – though it's a very charming pig I must say. Why do you suppose skittlers are always presumed to keep pigs? I see no essential connection between the two activities.

And they agree to ask Reeves to perform the opening ceremony. Muriel is also quick to realize that Reeves could be useful to Pat, who is hoping to get an exhibition at the New Dimension Gallery and is due to ring up at any minute with news about it. Every point in the plot is made to bear on every other.

Bolt strikes a nice balance in making Winifred silly but sympathetic in her attitude to patronage:

> Well, I do believe that people like me, who have no Creative Ability themselves, who contribute nothing to the Culture of Society in which they live, are passengers. ... Yes, passengers. And it is their Duty to help the Artist in any way they can.

She has been helping Pat by over-paying Muriel for her rather vague job. But William, who hasn't painted since he came to Budmouth, is obviously jealous of the unsuccessful young man.

Pat is in some ways a blueprint for Louis in *The Tiger and the Horse*. Instead of ringing, he arrives with the news that the gallery isn't interested, and talks bitterly and disparagingly about his talent with something of the self-pity that comes into Louis when he talks about his class. And his long speech about texture shows a venomous hostility to the Establishment, represented by the gallery.

Robert Bolt

You know what they mean by texture, don't you – 'A little bit of
oil – not too much turps – a stipple of red oxide, and then just –
pluck up the surface with a white chalk – pluck pluck pluck – *oh*
interesting. ... You know that one of the barn – where is it –
here. No texture there either. 'Now take this wall; this wall', he
said, 'this old stone.' 'It isn't old stone,' I said. 'It's paint. Water
and pigment on a flat piece of paper.' Well then he said I was a
formalist and that formalism was on the way out. But his buddy
said I used perspective so I couldn't be a formalist. That foxed
'em ... You were wrong about the suit too, Mule. Artists are
wearing dark grey this season, with a slit up the back.

The major structural resemblance to *The Circle* is in the way the
experience of the younger couple repeats that of the older. Muriel
wants Pat to get a job now that there's no hope of making money
from an exhibition and with a baby coming she won't be able to go
on working: when he adamantly refuses, it looks as though he's going
to be just as unscrupulously parasitic on her as William has been on
Winifred. But there are transverse lines across the parallelogram too.
Winifred overhears Muriel's plaintive speech about the biscuit-barrel
full of bills and not having a pair of shoes for the winter. It looks as
though her patronage of the arts will be extended more positively
towards Pat.

Bolt has already acquired the technique of making each entrance
count dramatically. Through coming in unseen by the others, Winifred
overhears something which is liable to make her intervene financially,
and after she's come back in tears from William's room, the doctor
comes back. Unable to hide her tears, she tries to blame them on the
fact that she can't move the table: he helps her and the business
covers their ensuing conversation. Altogether Bolt is adroit at making
dramatic capital out of eccentricity, which justifies moments of
explicitness and insight, abrupt shifts of mood and obstinate unreasonableness, as when she refuses to discuss the possibility of taking
a holiday in London.

Reeves enters just as they are quarrelling but it relaxes the surface
tension as they all look at the book he's brought as a present for
Winifred, but immediately there's suspense again as Potter enters
from the house and violently gestures to make Barret comes inside to

see William. Left alone with Winifred, Reeves flips through Pat's portfolio and immediately remarks on his indifference to texture. Reeves has been waging a campaign about texture in his weekly column and he claims that the galleries are now catching on. When Potter and Barret have a scene together, we learn that William has just had a stroke but the doctor doesn't want Winifred to be told because she's on the verge of breakdown herself. William could die any day or he could last for years. Potter reveals that he has just made a new will which affects Winifred, and then the strands in the plot are woven even more tightly together when we learn that Reeves is on the committee that awards a scholarship which could save Pat from all his financial difficulties and, just before the act ends, we hear that he's writing a biography of William. Bolt may have had recourse to some rather worn story cornerstones (like a will) but for someone so new to the theatre it's an astonishingly accomplished first act. Even the two professional men are personally involved in the plot which draws the other four so closely together and the dying man off stage makes his presence very palpably felt.

From the black dress Muriel is wearing at the beginning of Act Two and from Reeves's black tie, we infer that William is dead and from their conversation it soon becomes clear that the new will is spiteful – Winifred may no longer be able to afford to run the house. When we see Winifred, she seems suspiciously calm, but when the doctor comes Reeves asks him whether the shock of the will is holding down the effects of the shock of the death. She knows the contents of the will but hasn't yet had it read to her. Potter arrives to read it and tries to persuade her to contest it, but she refuses. He's left everything except the house to be divided between three galleries, and the will goes on:

> I leave the house to my sister since I believe the expenditure of initiative necessary to a removal would be fatal to her. I do not leave my money to her since the function of money is the enlargement of life, and she has demonstrated that she has no capacity for life. I do not intend that my money, for which I worked long and hard, should pass to the use of strangers; and her insatiable lust for self-sacrifice would inevitably result in its being enjoyed by people whom I have never seen, and have therefore no desire to make happy.

Winifred reacts by weeping and wanting to sleep. It is at this moment that Pat swoops down on her, cryptically demanding one of William's suits, but it's not till he's left alone with her that we find out the reason. He's got the chance of a job at a local hotel as a waiter if he provides his own tails.

Perhaps the chief fault in the play is that the plot works too well. The various points in the story all interrelate with such close precision that the interrelationships take up all the time and all the space without leaving Bolt any elbow room to exploit his richly dramatic material, except by preparing for the next phase in the plot's development. Winifred's character is the most interesting and he does give her slightly more emotional breathing space than the others. She suffers touchingly after hearing the will and her self–denying generosity is almost irritating.

> WINIFRED : I'm fifty-five, Newton! I've had my life.
> REEVES : That isn't so, my dear; you haven't had your life. You've twenty years to come, and the wisdom you have acquired from so much self-sacrifice —
> WINIFRED : Self-sacrifice! Wisdom! Oh Newton I feel wounded. I feel as though someone had shot a bullet through me. I daren't move . . . I'm being silly. Newton, can't you give that Scholarship to Pat ? I'm so afraid he'll get bitter if you don't.

The character and the situation are both so well contrived that she can carry the plot forward by importuning Reeves about Pat at the same time as displaying her own exorbitant selflessness. And at the moment of trying to give an honest answer to the question of whether she's been a fool or William a villain, she shows the extent to which she still romanticizes him, even after what's happened.

> I wasn't a coward! I *wanted* my life! And William knew. Oh it was wicked and shallow to say such things. He *was* a villain! . . . But he wasn't. I knew him and he wasn't. I've never known anyone so gentle as he was and he understood everything. It was harder for him to receive than it was for me to give. At one time.

And in this scene, where comparatively little happens, the language becomes more fanciful and less colloquial.

REEVES: You thought of me as successful. I know. And so I am. But it's not what I wanted, Winifred. If I look back – I cannot remember what my motives were, nor those of all the people I knew. They are like figures in an open air play, at the far side of a park.

And it's touching when Winifred speaks of the man who wept when she wouldn't marry him:

REEVES: When was this my dear?
WINIFRED: February the 7th, 1929. It was raining and I had a cold and oh I remember every detail!

The whole play becomes much more deeply involving here as she speaks of being her brother's 'Bride in Art'. He used to fall in love with every girl he met but never had the courage to approach them and just talked to her about it. She brings in a bundle of William's copies of the love letters he wrote and she takes a photograph of him and herself out of her handbag and tears it down the middle, saying that he used to call it their wedding photograph. Then plot takes over again. When Barret arrives with William's things, Reeves pockets the letters while Winifred is inside the house and then, looking at his manuscript, which William has been reading just before he died, he finds a hand-written note in it cancelling the will and leaving everything to Winifred on condition she gives nothing away. And neatly, the turn in the financial tide comes just in time to save Pat from having to be a waiter. Still more neatly, the act ends with a reversion to the *status quo*. Potter arrives with the news that William had nothing to leave.

Act Three begins with the reproachful reactions of the doctor and the solicitor to Reeves's article which has now appeared in the Sunday paper, implying that William was impotent. This is the use he has made of the love letters. What creates more tension is that Winifred has now given William's portraits of her, which are the only things she has of any value, to Pat, and she implores Reeves to give him the scholarship, so that he'll no longer need them. Reeves's conversation with Pat, as he examines his portfolio, is to be another *scene à faire* but before it comes we see Muriel trying unsuccessfully to pressure Pat into promising to give back the portraits, whatever Reeves

Robert Bolt

decides. Bolt makes a good deal out of the big scene when it comes. Reeves says no, but it's a regretful no, and he's encouraging to Pat, though he advises him that he's not ready for an exhibition. It's good that he's contemptuous of Reeves's advice, but he doesn't altogether ring true as a painter.

> It isn't just that. I work at this stuff. As far back as I could do anything, it's painting I've done. When other blokes are earning nice clothes for their wives to wear – I paint! When other blokes have got their feet up – I paint! When other blokes are getting themselves a future or having themselves a time – I paint! When other blokes are doing anything – I'm painting! I tell you I've done enough! I've earned something! Where is it?

And from the way he talks of moments that moved him to paint, he sounds like a very bad painter. 'Okay, I know it's corny,' he says of a feeling he had after coming out of the National Gallery in November when the lights were on and the girls were coming out of the offices.

> PAT: I felt . . . terrific.
> REEVES: Everyone feels like that sometimes, Pat.
> PAT: But this is the difference. The difference. When I got home I got – I got that – piece of paper and I (*his voice is unsteady with the effort to express: his hand makes violent but constricted gestures with spread fingers*) I – put – the paint – on!

But Bolt obviously means us to take Pat seriously as having a real, if undeveloped, talent.

Whatever his merits as a painter, his merit as a man is tested in the next *scene à faire,* when, egged on by Muriel, he talks to Winifred about giving the portraits back. Weakly, and playing unscrupulously on her extreme susceptibility to the cause of Art and the Artist, he leads her on into suggesting a compromise – for him to sell the pictures and give her fifty per cent of what he gets for them.

Will Muriel be able to dissuade him from taking advantage of the old lady? And will she allow Reeves to keep the letters which he says he needs for the book? (Now – as all through the play – the issues resolve themselves into conflicts which must be played out between two alternative courses of action which affect the fates and fortunes of the protagonists. And Bolt has gone on writing like this, which is why he has been at his best with raw material that lends itself to Either/Or treatment.) On these two points, Winifred goes on playing her chosen role as victim, unable now, as she always has been, to insist on her rights or even to accept what's offered to her. The only point she insists on – and here too Bolt cleverly manages his plot so that the emotional drive can be focused on to a single concrete object – is that both halves of the torn photograph should be printed in Reeves's book.

FLOWERING CHERRY

Flowering Cherry was produced at the Haymarket in November 1957 with Sir Ralph Richardson as Cherry, Celia Johnson as his wife, Isobel, and Andrew Ray as their son Tom. It ran for over a year till December 1958.

Bolt himself criticized the play as being uneasily straddled between naturalism and non-naturalism. He says he had 'a dreadful struggle to get over into non-naturalism. In *Flowering Cherry* I tried it by dumping here and there a big poetic speech and extra-natural effects of music and vision. The result was a kind of uneasy wobble, which presented the actors and the director with hellish problems.'*

I should have said that the basic difficulties lay more in the subject-matter than in the form. The characters themselves are intrinsically far more ordinary and far less interesting than the characters in *The Critic and the Heart* – a frustrated insurance salesman, his emotionally under-nourished wife and their two problem children. And whereas one of the most interesting features of *The Critic and the Heart* was the way in which the characters were made interdependent, here we are dealing with a family, which means that the basic tensions between them are inevitably close to tensions which have been exploited dramatically over and over again. And it's hard to make commonplace material dramatically meaningful by the methods of head-on confrontation and direct viewpoint clashes which Bolt used in *The Critic and the Heart* and uses again here. Although the situation, as before, is well worked out to provide climacteric conflicts, many of the arguments between the characters sound like commonplace family rows in which each member of the family attacks each of the others in turn, partly for character weaknesses and partly for a viewpoint which results largely from his or her being in that position in the family. For commonplace characters to be made interesting in a commonplace situation, a technique is needed which ploughs well into the undersoil.

In one way Sir Ralph was helping the play by giving such a big

*Encore, March–April 1961. Interview with the Editors.

performance as such a small man. As Kenneth Tynan said in his *Observer* review,

> He is interesting all the time, without respite; even when he plays a dull man, that dull man is never permitted a dull moment. Sir Ralph will spruce him up and set him frisking, running the gamut from manic to depressive; the fellow's neuroses will get a thorough airing, as if they were dogs being taken out for a walk. Everything about him will be written, in a flowing hand, all over Sir Ralph's face, and his simplest remark will seem eccentric when the Richardson voice, waltzing and skating from syllable to syllable, has finished with it.

But in another way, as Tynan went on to say, Sir Ralph was damaging the play. He was upsetting the balance with the other characters and he was even upsetting Bolt's balance between the reality and the fantasy in Cherry's life.

Like Winifred, who went against Nature by staying a spinster, Cherry has gone against Nature by staying in the office. Bolt's hatred of the whole ethos is summed up in his description of Gilbert Grass, the man who's going to get Cherry's job when he's sacked.

> *He is an undersized, bespectacled man with a face boldly designed to express fear, but wearing the covert confidence of those not hampered by self-respect. Either he was formed by Nature for office life or office life has formed his nature; either way he is a condemnation of it.*

Sir Ralph's Cherry was altogether too big a man to be contained in such a little life. It's hard enough, anyway, even from the script, to imagine this man staying for twenty years inside the day-to-day routine of the insurance office.

> But I can't, I can't give myself to a job like that. Those green lampshades every morning and that blasted rubber carpet! D'you know what it makes me think of?
> GRASS (*ready to take the joke*): No?
> CHERRY: It's like walking on corpses.

It's clear enough how his hatred of office life drives Cherry into fantasies about buying an orchard in Somerset, but it might have produced a more fully rounded and more credible picture of him if we'd actually seen him in conversation with his office boss, instead of just hearing his distorted accounts of the conversations. Certainly we see from his behaviour at home that he can very easily be cowed but, as it is, the best indication we get of the other side of his ambivalence about the office is his vacillation in his conversations with Isobel. When she tries to find out whether he's really handed in his notice, he's maddeningly evasive, hinting that he has, trying to find out whether she would like him to, and finally revealing that he hasn't.

Bolt juggles very deftly in this scene between Isobel's anxiety and the other emotional tension he has set up: the strained relationship between Cherry and Tom. It's when Tom gets his father angry that he starts lying about having given notice. Bolt is also deft in conveying the quality of Cherry's relationships with the other characters through his attitudes towards them: patronizing boastfulness to Grass, exasperation at Tom, immature emotional dependence on Isobel.

As in *The Critic and the Heart*, Bolt situates all his characters at moments when developments are imminent which will be crucial. Cherry is on the verge of losing his job, Isobel's tolerance of him is at breaking point, Tom is about to be called up for National Service, and Judy, the design student daughter, seems to be on the point of leaving home to share a flat with an attractive friend, Carol. It's doubtful how she'll be able to pay for it but she says she's going to get an award. Later we find out that she's inherited her father's proclivity to counting unhatched chickens, and Carol drops her when the award goes to another student.

For Cherry, the real crunch comes when he gets a chance of realizing his dream and selling the house to buy an orchard. And for Isobel, his cowardly refusal to take the chance clinches her decision to leave him for the sympathetic salesman who arrives at the house because Cherry has been writing to his firm about apple trees.

Almost always, a play uses specific objects which become nearly symbolic because of action which hinges on them and in *Flowering Cherry* the central objects are the two pokers. Cherry is always talking about Jesse Bishop, the massively strong farm labourer who could bend the thicker one and he shows off himself by bending the thinner one, challenging Tom to straighten it. He makes a desperate effort to bend the thicker one when Carol offers to reward him with a kiss but he collapses into a chair with a 'dizzy spell' and at the end of the play he kills himself by struggling with it, after telling Isobel that he's doing it for her and convincing himself insanely that she'll stay if he succeeds. Ironically, she has already left by the time he makes his major effort. The theatrical effectiveness of the pokers was rather reduced by the fact that there had to be two of them and the effect which translated Cherry's dying vision into a stage picture could never have succeeded because it involved a change of convention at the very last minute. The rear wall had been painted on a scrim and when light came up behind it, we saw an orchard through it.

The on-stage object which does make a valid and valuable contribution to the action and atmosphere is the barrel of scrumpy, the rough cider which Cherry drinks and tries to inflict on all his guests, though Carol is the only one who claims to like it. Good use is made of the barrel in the scene where they rather flirt together as he shows her how to work the tap and generally it serves as a constant, solid reminder of Cherry's fantasy life. And when he's sacked and gets drunk on scrumpy laced with gin, there's a very good moment when Isobel, making a pathetic attempt at reconciliation during one of their rows, tries to drink out of his glass.

The weakest passages in the play are passages of argument when we might be listening to any father and any son, or any husband and any wife. When, for instance, Cherry is showing his Philistinism and attacking his son's professed enthusiasm for modern art. Or when he's warning him about army life:

> My word, boy, you've got a rude awakening coming; they'll teach you quick enough in the army. I only hope you get an RSM like one or two I've known. There's no State Scholarships there.

And again in the scene with Tom in Act Two, when his father's giving him advice about girls and telling him that a man gets no pleasure with them in bed unless he respects them, the scene suffers from the fact that it's attempting nearly exactly the same kind of father–son confrontation that we've seen hundreds of times before on the stage, though here at least it's partly redeemed by the irony. Cherry is

27

warning Tom that Carol is 'rather a common type of girl' after we've
seen his behaviour with her when they're alone together.

Judy is the most unusual member of the family but she's the least
developed. Her first entrance makes a strong impact, quickly estab-
lishing her disapproval of her father. We see that she lumps him
together with the mess he makes in the house and we see the vicious-
ness in her dislike when she tidies the room, throwing beer bottles into
the dustbin, even when Isobel tells her that there's money on them.
From the way that she speaks about the unreliable Carol, it's clear
that she's transferred to her all the emotional loyalty that she no
longer invests in the family. But the use that Bolt makes of Judy in
the action doesn't enable him to penetrate very usefully or very
interestingly into her problems. The chief point comes when, blaming
her father for Carol's defection, Judy, despite Tom's attempts to
hold her back, denounces Cherry to Isobel for trying to kiss Carol.

Developing Judy's part in the action might also have helped to
make *Flowering Cherry* less reminiscent of *Death of a Salesman*, for
there's no daughter in that. It's not only that Cherry's difficulties
with money are similar and that the central relationships are similar
with the firm that shows no appreciation for length of service, with
the wife who does her best to defend Father against the children and
with the children who lose their very last vestiges of faith in him – but
the tone is sometimes similar too. Isobel's speech demanding respect
for Cherry is rather like Linda's famous speech insisting that 'attention must be paid' to such a man as Willy Loman.

> Your father wants to be a farmer. He hates the job; he's always
> wanted to be a farmer. You have no idea how much that means
> to him. He hates it and he's done it for you. For you, do you
> understand! He's been through a great deal and he's a fine man in
> all sorts of ways and you will treat him with respect! With
> respect! With respect! With respect!
> (*She puts her face in her hands and weeps. Tom and Judy regard
> her, guilty and embarrassed.*)

But the language here is rather flat and feeble and it's not clear
whether we're meant to regard Isobel as feeble at this point. Arthur
Miller's language for Linda's speech is not at all impressive, but it's
quite clear that our sympathies are meant to be with her.

The scene between Isobel and the children altogether seems rather forced. Judy's mention of the £3,000 salary earned by one of the previous winners of the design award is used to touch off a general conversation about Cherry's income and assets. Looking around at the kitchen, Tom says 'They can't pay him much,' but we aren't convinced that this could really be the first time it had struck him. It's one of the eternal problems of naturalism, finding a way for characters to comment on their own situation without going outside it. Here Bolt gets much nearer to finding a temporary solution when he introduces Bowman, the salesman, as a catalyst: it's effective when Isobel is put on the spot in Tom's presence over Cherry's correspondence with the growers about apple trees for an orchard he hasn't got.

There's also some amiable writing in the scene after this, when she tries to have it out with Cherry. They can still surprise each other and move each other after twenty-five years together, and here, as in *A Man for All Seasons* and *The Tiger and the Horse,* Bolt is very good at getting the mercury in the marital thermometer to jump up and down as the husband and wife sometimes succeed and sometimes fail at getting through to each other. But though the dialogue sensitively reflects the nature of Cherry's and Isobel's mutual involvement, it loses its quality when it tumbles back into the basics – which just because they're so basic are also commonplace: how long is it since they've slept together? What did the boss say in the office row? In any case, the scene makes it quite clear enough that the central issue in the play is going to be whether the marriage can survive, without pointing it quite so explicitly at the curtain to Act One, when Isobel, alone in the garden, cries out 'Let me leave him,' while she overhears Cherry indoors reciting the prologue to *Henry V* to impress Carol.

Unfortunately the device on which Bolt chiefly depended to lift the play above a commonplace level was the long speeches, and though they're convincing enough, there isn't really enough texture or substance in the writing for them to take us any further than the shorter speeches do.

CHERRY: That's right. He was the Lord of the Harvest, as they used to call him in those days. Oh, harvest time was something glorious then, the horses and the men. They used to bring up huge parcels of bread from the farm, a perfect mountain of bread, and real Cheddar cheese, and cold boiled bacon under the hedge on a tablecloth; the dogs used to sit round in a circle with their tongues hanging out, the dogs the men brought, terriers and collies, they came from miles for the rats, the hares and rabbits in the corn. The dogs my father had were beautiful. From our big field you looked right over the Plain of Somerset; nothing but pasture and orchards, it's too wet for crops, it's not much above sea level; green and blue as far as you could see. The men were a rough lot and I wasn't much better than the men, but the place was something all right ... The way those old-time squires planted trees – there was an avenue of elm trees two miles long that didn't go anywhere; it's still there, I'll bet; ecclesiastical property, they won't have cut it down. That's another thing we could see up there, the old cathedral. They used to set their watches by the bells and my father said, 'Allow nine seconds for the distance.' It's a noble pile, that building, a gem of architecture; yes, many's the time you could bend down and look between your legs – (*he does it*) – with the sweat running into your eyes – (*he rises*) – and see this thing the Normans built, crumbling away like something soft in the sunshine we had then ... We were as brown as – pieces of furniture!

It's interesting that the reference to Jesse Bishop as Lord of the Harvest foreshadows the development of this theme in *Gentle Jack* but the whole speech is like something you might overhear in a pub, and while it's no doubt the way Cherry would speak, this doesn't help to find a focus which can take in both the inadequate man and the beautiful dream. His attack of dizziness after he tries to bend the thicker poker for Carol can be very effective in the hands of an actor like Sir Ralph, and the family quarrel about the missing two pounds, which Cherry has stolen out of Isobel's bag provides useful theatrical suspense. There's a particularly neat use of the altercation when Tom opens his call-up papers in the middle of it:

> TOM: Why? Explain why it's worse to suspect him than me. (*Picking up letter.*) Is this my call-up?
> ISOBEL: I hope so!
> TOM (*opens it*): Congratulate yourself. It is.

ISOBEL (*a little faint*): Oh, Tom. Is it?
(*Tom shows it.*)
TOM: Don't spoil it! I'm *half* emancipated now – keep it up a bit and you'll have a man in the house.

The action builds up to considerable tension when it looks doubtful whether Isobel will ever find out that it's Cherry who took the money. The crisis when she does is exploited well, but this time her showdown scene with Cherry, who has now lost his job, borders on sentimentality.

ISOBEL (*approaching, quietly coaxing*): Jim, tell me the truth about one thing. *Why* did you take it?
CHERRY: Well, I was short. (*Bracing a little.*) There's none in the bank, Bel.
ISOBEL (*gently*): No?
CHERRY (*bracing a little more*): Bel, I —
ISOBEL (*encouraging, hopeful*): Yes?
CHERRY (*failing*): We've overspent, I suppose.
ISOBEL: The *truth*, Jim! Oh, why can't you say – (*She cries out*) – 'I lost my job!'
CHERRY (*stares at her in silence*): You know? (*He sits, puts one hand before his face. He speaks with the tremendous weak happiness that follows confession.*) Thank God, thank God you know. (*He puts the other hand over his face, sobs.*) O-o-o-o-o-o-oh.
(*Isobel walks jerkily up and down behind him, regarding his shaking back, moved to him but too tired to be certain.*)
ISOBEL (*cautious*): Jim?
CHERRY (*controls his eagerness for reconciliation*): Yes?
(*He half peeps behind his fingers. He sniffs. One hand moves out automatically for the little parcel.*)
ISOBEL (*springing upon him and knocking it off the table*): LEAVE your knife alone! (*It clatters to the floor.*) (*Rages.*) You see? You can't even weep! You're lying now! Everything you do is a lie! You're lying all the time! There's absolutely *nothing* you have any respect for! Nothing! Your apples and orchards; your dreams; your one dream – it's nothing but a lie and an excuse for lies and lies! You can't even weep!

But it's a very well-made play. Judy's accusation that Cherry has mauled Carol about comes just at the right point in the scene between husband and wife. We see how readily Isobel would discount the incident before the play proceeds to the slightly too clean-cut issues with which it ends. Grass comes back with the offer of a rather inferior agency, which Cherry must either accept or reject. Isobel states her terms for staying with him: either he must sell the house and buy an orchard or take the agency and lose her. Like Sir Thomas More and like Jacko in *Gentle Jack*, Cherry dies because he can't survive in face of the Either/Or that he's presented with.

THE TIGER AND THE HORSE

The Tiger and the Horse didn't open in London until August 24th 1960 but it was written before *A Man for All Seasons,* which had opened at the Globe on July 1st. *The Tiger and the Horse* ran at the Queen's Theatre till March 1961 while *A Man for All Seasons* ran at the Globe till April.

It would be misleading to call *The Tiger and the Horse* a play about the bomb, but a petition against it provides a crucial issue and the petition itself is an object which plays a large role in the action. The central question is whether the wife of a Master of a College, who is likely to succeed as Vice-Chancellor of the University, should sign it, as she wants to, or bow to considerations of her husband's career. It's interesting that the people who pressure her not to sign are all more likeable than Louis, the organizer of the petition, who has the right ideas and the wrong motivations. Bolt uses his characters' well differentiated attitudes to the petition and to the other events in the central line of action to explore them, but the individuals rather seem to be built round the attitudes they express. The play raises a number of important moral questions which the characters have to face and discuss, but though the discussion is cleverly harnessed to pull the action along with it, the writing is nothing like as effective in animating the characters as it is in defining their viewpoints.

Like *Flowering Cherry, The Tiger and the Horse* is very well constructed. The parts are skilfully pieced together so that each element in the plot develops and influences the development of each of the other elements. And at the end of the play, when the Master's wife, Gwendoline, who has been poised throughout on the verge of madness, topples over and loses all control, the logic of the play's argument about responsibility fuses completely with the story and much of the third act is very moving.

The characters are all more intellectual and articulate than in *Flowering Cherry,* which largely justifies the kind of self-consciousness that Bolt creates in them. They are better entitled than the Cherrys to comment on themselves and their situations as from outside, but, particularly in Act One, the plot steers them into shallows which have been navigated all too many times before. Stella, the younger daughter of Jack and Gwendoline Dean, is in love with Louis but thinks it's wrong to go to bed with him. We get a scene in which her elder sister Mary advises her how to make herself attractive and how to dragoon Louis into marrying her, and we get several scenes with Louis, talking about the moral problems and the practical dangers.

Oddly enough, both Louis and Stella are characterized far more tellingly in the stage directions which introduce them than in the opening dialogue between them, most of which is used to build up to Jack Dean's entrance. As before, manipulation of the craftsmanlike plot is crowding exploration of character and exploitation of material into too confined a space. We learn that Jack was an F.R.S. before he was thirty and changed from astronomy to philosophy when he was forty, which makes him sound extremely interesting, but, like many of the points in the stage directions, these facts are never exploited as they might be. Similarly with Hugo Slate, the present Vice-Chancellor, it's interesting to read that the academic life is his only possible element, but though this is a point which could be developed dramatically, it isn't. There's so much potentially good material in the plot that much of it has to be wasted through being developed in terms of either/or situations, and with a bevy of distinguished minds in the cast of characters, it's a pity that the plot constricts their functioning so much. Many of the scenes have the effect of just giving us the headlines about a situation before passing on to another subject. Not that Bolt is uninterested in his characters, but he constantly passes up chances of showing their minds really getting to grips with a subject in order to seize chances of strengthening and quickening his story line. The issue of whether Gwendoline should sign the petition appears to be complicated by Jack's prospects of being appointed to the Vice-Chancellorship; in fact the complication works dangerously like a simplification.

Often we get tantalizing hints of subjects which could have been developed fascinatingly, as when Gwendoline feels that she's responsible for Mary's lack of ability and Stella's lack of discipline. Like Judy, the loneliest character in *Flowering Cherry*, Gwendoline, who is the loneliest in *The Tiger and the Horse*, is the most interesting and the

least developed. The growth of her madness could have well occupied
the central position in the play, but it gets roped too tightly to the
issue of the petition and the bomb and it sinks under the surface until
it asserts itself in a big action – when she slashes the college Holbein.
In Act One she's also rather obscured by her husband, who gives us a
foretaste of Sir Thomas More when he makes a show of refusing to
coerce her in any way for the sake of his own advancement. We get
another hint of saintliness in his character when Sir Hugo Slate, talking of Gwendoline's father, who 'in the evening of his days subsisted
almost entirely upon oats' asks whether he wasn't a saint. 'Don't say
that,' Dean answers, 'I am reputed to resemble him.' And there's
another curious hint in Act Two when Stella speaks to her father about
a crown of thorns:

> DEAN: What was that about some old woman on the train?
> STELLA: Oh! She was one of those very smart old women – she
> must have been way past fifty, but really quite sexy; and she
> was wearing a pretty hat with a bird in it.
> DEAN (*softly, looking down at her*): Yes?
> STELLA: Only it was that awful Friday evening train and after
> about an hour she fell asleep. And her face began to look – like
> yours when you're asleep. (*He uncrosses his legs restlessly.*) No
> really this isn't imagination – everyone in the compartment
> was watching her. And by the time we got into town, this little
> hat looked like a crown of thorns.

But this saintly quality in Dean only comes clearly into focus when
he movingly gives his mad wife his full support in Act Three. In Act
One he pleads ignorance of the 'diplomatic and military considerations'
involved in the problem of the bomb, and the question of whether
he's justified in doing this is only touched in passing. The question
in the foreground here is that of Louis's relationship with the family.
The point lies less in what Louis is saying than in his offensive manner
of saying it and altogether the plot strands are woven together so well
that the individual strands are liable to choke for want of breathing
space.

In Act Two, Louis's relationships with Stella and with the family
are still very much in the foreground and his offensiveness soon comes
to make him sound like a belated reincarnation of Jimmy Porter,

Robert Bolt

though the comedy that deflates his inverted snobbery partly compensates for his tiresomeness.

> LOUIS: I apologize. I apologize. (*He backs about the stage bowing at the word 'apologize'.*) I apologize for wearing the wrong sort of clothes and for making it worse with the wrong sort of face; I apologize for my opinions and my table manners. (*He works himself up in self-pity.*) If I smell, as I dare say I do, I apologize for that. In short I apologize for having a father who worked for the Gas Company and a mother who ... (*voice now trembling with self-pity; this is his prize-exhibit*). My mother died of malnutrition!
>
> MARY (*dryly*): She died last year of pneumonia.
> LOUIS: Of malnutrition!
> MARY: Of pneumonia. Stella told me.
> LOUIS (*stopped short; then coming back with defensive aggression*): People don't die of pneumonia if they've been properly fed!

There are three long speeches in Act Two which stand out clearly from the rest of the action: the first is Sir Hugo's description of flying in his son's plane.

> DEAN (*smiling*): Tell us about it.
> SLATE: That is my intention. (*Commences his set piece.*) My most vivid impression is of personal discomfort. One is swaddled in straps and secured to a thing like an apple-barrel. This is an ejector-seat and allegedly contains a parachute. The pilot – my son in this case – then operates the levers and one is whisked into the atmosphere like a falling stone – only upwards, of course. There is also (*flutters his fingers in front of his face*) a species of rubber tea-cosy the purpose of which eluded me throughout. The noise is not loud but curiously unfriendly, and the whole accompanied by a gentle shaking motion (*he holds hands before him and imitates the motion of shaking something down into a sock*), well calculated to unhinge. (*Sits.*) Not for any consideration would I repeat the experience. But experience it undoubtedly is. The interior of those machines is of a complexity — (*He gestures helplessly.*) They live in a different world, Jack.

This is pleasant and amusing in a quiet way but it's more like an interlude than something which helps the main action.

The second is much better and much more useful. It comes from Louis when Stella asks him whether he'd still want to marry her if it weren't for the baby.

LOUIS: Oh, Stella, who can say?
STELLA: You.
LOUIS (*throughout this speech he paces jerkily about while she sits, motionless. He clings desperately to the forms of logic while the emotion of which he is ashamed forces through*): No I can't, no one can. I mean, if the circumstances weren't what the circumstances are, then for one thing I wouldn't be me and you wouldn't be you. You pregnant are a different person from you not pregnant. I mean you as you are now are a person I've asked to marry me – a person I *want* to marry me ... It may be because – well no not *because* – but one of the things about you at the moment happens to be that you — (STELLA *is silent. He recommences with fresh funds of reasonableness but descends quickly into distress.*) What I mean is, I've asked you to and therefore I must want you to. Otherwise why should I have asked you? A person does what he wants to do. It's a proof that he wants to do it that he did it. That's inescapable, it's a matter of definition. I can't pretend – it's not to be expected – that I'm entirely, just *happy* now, because – Oh hell! Let's leave it!

The jerkiness that the stage direction prescribes is well reflected in the rhythm of the writing and it communicates not just that he's ambivalent but also that he's hedging. He finds it much more difficult to be honest about the baby than he does about the bomb. But he's under pressure and the attitude is pressure-cooked. Too often in this play the attitude comes out raw and the situation is cooked to contain it.

The last long speech is not nearly so successful. Stella is bravely determined to have the baby without marrying a man who doesn't really want her, and in an evening scene with her father and a telescope, she takes some comfort from the stability of a system in which all the planets have been going round the sun for a thousand million years.

STELLA: Cor! I'd like to be up there tonight.

Robert Bolt

DEAN: You would not.

STELLA *(swinging the telescope slightly)*: Isn't it dark *between* the stars?

DEAN *(looking at them, starts quietly and gradually increases speed)*: So dark, that if you were up there, a candle would look like sheet lightning; so silent, that an echo would be as solid as a bank; so ignorant of human necessities, that the smell of a single privet leaf would riot through your senses like an orgy! And for all your endless gliding at a million miles an hour you would be more static than the hands of a stopped clock. Oh yes, the moons go round the planets and the planets go round the sun and the sun goes round the Milky Way, but that doesn't matter because the Milky Way is circling round itself as it goes looping from nowhere to nowhere and in twenty-four billion years the sun will be back where it started. None of it matters since happily it leaves no trace, but if all the galaxies were God's Fingers Dipped in Light d'you know what pattern they would make? Scribble! . . . *(He is breathing hard. On a note of going.)* So if you find them comforting *(pointing rather unsteadily at the telescope)* now's the time to stop. *(Puts on coat.)*

This is not very convincing as coming from an ex-astronomer with an outstanding mind. The language would be acceptable if the intention were to put Dean in focus as talking in a self-consciously poetic way, but it isn't. The imagery is only very loosely anchored down and the use of language is both unscientific and uneconomic. The word 'orgy' partly repeats the sense of the word 'riot', and 'stopped' repeats 'static', without there being any appearance of calculated point in the overlaps. What's more important is that the brightly coloured conceits sap away the force of the main point which comes at the end. The self-intoxicated metaphors and similes, which are worthy of Christopher Fry, provide quite the wrong build-up to this profoundly pessimistic point about total lack of pattern in the universe.

What is valuable, though, is the contrast between the impression of spaciousness with which this scene ends Act Two and the sudden constriction which faces us at the beginning of Act Three. We are moved to an untidy flat full of makeshift furniture, high up in a Victorian house on the edge of the town, with nappies airing in front of a

Sir Ralph Richardson as Cherry in the Haymarket Theatre production of *Flowering Cherry* with Susan Burnet as Carol

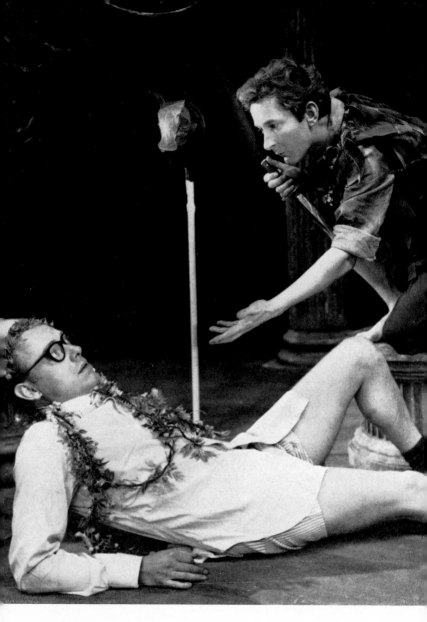

Michael Bryant and Kenneth Williams as Jacko and Jack in *Gentle Jack* at the Queen's Theatre

small electric fire. It's a far cry from the night sky studied at leisure in a don's garden and, significantly, the telescope which Stella has brought with her is canted down in a position of disuse. Stella herself has changed.

> *She has changed for the better and worse, is a more considerable, less immediately likeable person than she was. Her generosity is overlaid by a manner somewhat brittle and censorious. Her clothes are much better – rather consciously sober, but dignified and becoming; hair pulled back, long dark skirt, plain black jumper, brown scarf. The basis of it all is still her youthfulness.*

But this time it's not just a matter of what the stage direction specifies: the change is borne out in her dialogue and above all in her manner to Louis. She is less dependent on him in proportion as she is maturer. His speech to her through the closed door is a good gloss on his development and a good milestone to mark how far he has come since his long speech in Act Two. Rejected, he has become pathetic and it's satisfying to see the cocky lover deflated into the abject father wooing the woman who has borne his child:

> I've switched the fire off, Stella! (*No answer. He goes to door of bedroom.*) You left it on. (*No answer. He tries the handle.*) Stella, you left the fire on. (*Listens. On a note of laughing protest, as though this were all a little joke*) Hey, Stella! ... (*No answer. Injured.*) Stella! ... (*No answer.*) Is Fred all right? (*No answer.*) I only want to see Fred! (*No answer. He puts down the books, extracts an exercise book, opens it at a certain page.*) Stella, I've got something to show you! (*No answer. He rattles the door knob. Becoming distracted and his voice rising*) Stella, please let me in! (*No answer. He suddenly pounds the door, leaning on it, almost weeping for all that is behind it.*) I want to see Fred! I want to see Fred! (*The baby, alarmed, begins to cry. He listens as the cries abruptly cease. Then, stooping, he folds up the paper and begins to push it under the door.* STELLA *opens the door quickly; she is carrying the baby. She is angry, but her anger is diminished to irritation by her surprise at seeing him on his hands and knees.*) It's a poem. (*Rises and offers it to her.*) It's a sonnet; I'm going to do a cycle. It's – I'd like to know what you think of it.

D

Robert Bolt

Much of the act is spent building up to Gwendoline's entrance. A series of telephone calls creates the feeling that something is very wrong, without explaining what, and then a visit from Sir Hugo brings us a description of how she has slashed the Holbein. There may have been better ways of approaching her madness than making her put a tea-cosy on her head, but the heightened language in her speech works incomparably better than that in Dean's speech about the sky.

> MRS DEAN: Yes. I wanted to. I told myself it was for Mr Flax's petition of Peace. But in fact I wanted to! I ripped across their little faces, and it rejoiced me! . . . Oh hypocrisy, thank God I've come to the end of you!
>
> DEAN (*his ordered manner becomes a shell in which his fear rattles audibly. Stiff faced*): 'Hyp — '? I fail to follow. What did you hope to achieve?
>
> STELLA: For Heaven's sake – are you blind!
>
> MRS DEAN (*smiles ruefully at* DEAN *as parents do at the youthful insensitivities of their children*): 'Blind' . . . . Your father knows, Stella. Better than anyone. (*To* DEAN, *smiling, comforting*) But give up now, dear. (*Looks at him. Then the same gentle smile.*) You forget, you are tormenting *me*, too.
>
> DEAN: Are you not well?
>
> MRS DEAN (*smiles round at the others, shaking her head*): He will never give up. (*Then*) He is a saint.

The speech, like the whole play, may rest explicitly or implicitly on black and white opposites – day and night, waking and dreaming, tiger and horse, goodness and evil, conscience and opportunism – but in providing a rational justification for departing from the reasonable and prosaic, the madness is enabling Bolt to write more freely than before. He sustains the level of the language very well, at the same time as using the scene to resolve the mystery of what had happened to the petition.

The climax which the madness precipitates is a good one. The shake it gives to the kaleidoscope produces a new perspective in which to judge all the main things that have happened. When Dean held out the fountain pen for Gwendoline to sign the petition, was he refusing to curb her liberty, as she insists, or was he subtly undermining it, as Stella insists? Or can it in some sense have been both? After her physical attack on him, the whole of their past relationship is in effect reassessed in the light of her asserton that he never liked her looks. Here the writing rises to a much higher level:

> When you touch me, I can *feel* the goodness in your fingers. Why even on our honeymoon I used to wonder, 'Why does he have to be so good, just to touch me?' And the answer – no. I didn't know the answer then, but I felt it get to its feet. Then later when you *talked* to me I could hear the goodness in your voice and I wondered. 'Why does he have to be good, just to talk to me?'
>
> DEAN: Not true!
>
> MRS DEAN: And the answer turned its head. ... Then I noticed even when I spoke to you, the patience in your face. 'Why must he be good just to listen to me?'
>
> DEAN: Not true!
>
> MRS DEAN: And it came towards me. 'Why does he never associate with me? Why have we never, never in anything been together?' And the answer. Sprang! ... Into the dreams, and when the dreams came into the day, I *was* the answer ... (*Desolute*) 'Gracious me,' I thought, 'a man who is the very lettering of sanity; married to me who have always been evil, and am now mad. No wonder he keeps what distance he can.

But plot takes over again at the last minute as the play slips into a conventional happy ending. The two least sympathetic characters – as they now seem – leave, Sir Hugo and the social-climbing elder sister. Dean jettisons all hope of even remaining Master, let alone becoming Vice-Chancellor, as he signs the petition himself, and by asking for his telescope back, indicates that he's going to return to astronomy. Louis finally convinces Stella that he loves her and they tell Dean that they're going to get married.

A MAN FOR ALL SEASONS

A Man for All Seasons has probably enjoyed more popularity than any other English play since the war. After a run of 320 performances in the West End, it was a great success on Broadway, where it was voted the Best Foreign Play of the Year (1962). Bolt himself wrote the screenplay, cutting out the part of the Common Man, although the director was in favour of keeping him. The film was made in 1966, with Paul Scofield playing Sir Thomas More, as he had on the stage both in London and New York. It won six academy awards and had long seasons in cinemas in many parts of the world.

In style, *A Man for All Seasons* is quite different from any of Bolt's previous plays, but it represents a continuation of the same line of thinking about behaviour. Cherry was a man who had so completely lost touch with his ideal that he was incapable of seizing a real chance of joining fantasy and reality together by selling the house and buying an orchard. Dean was basically a good man and though he'd turned a blind eye on some of the things going on around him and made certain moral compromises for the sake of climbing the academic ladder, he'd never got completely cut off from the ideal (which is represented partly by astronomy). And the action forces him to a point where he digs his heels in and shuts his ears to the counsels of opportunism (which are represented partly by Sir Hugo). *A Man for All Seasons* is a graph on which Bolt plots two curves: the steady rise of an opportunist and the decline of a man of principle.

At the beginning of the play, Richard Rich, who has studied Macchiavelli, is looking for a job. A graduate of Cambridge, he has been in London for seven months, which he has spent largely waiting about in ante-rooms. But he's contemptuous of More's offer to get him a post as a teacher. He's ambitious, and he's spineless, as we see from his chameleon efforts to please. In the presence of the Duke of Norfolk he's a name-dropping sycophant, but he lands a modest job in the Duke's household as librarian and then exploits his acquaintance with More to make himself useful to Cromwell, who needs information about him because he's been briefed by the King to make

More toe the line over the question of the divorce from Katherine of Aragon or, alternatively, to destroy him. Richard rises higher and higher socially as he stoops lower and lower morally, ending up as Sir Richard Rich, Attorney General for Wales, and a perjurer. His perjury supplies Cromwell with the 'evidence' he needs to discredit More and secure his death as a traitor. Rich is a man who can be pushed indefinitely without ever finding a point where he has to dig his heels in.

More, on the other hand, is a man who can't compromise beyond a certain point. He enjoys life, success, society, comfort and the King's friendship and he's quite adept at making the adjustments that a public figure has to make if he's to survive. At the beginning of the play, the curve of his career is still moving upwards. When Wolsey falls, it's More who succeeds him, but much as he wants to retain Henry's goodwill, conscience prevents him from giving his approval to the divorce when Henry is set on marrying Anne Boleyn. As Chancellor, More was involved in Henry's actions and he compromised by agreeing not to make his misgivings public. And he even accepted the Act of Supremacy which pronounced Henry 'Supreme Head of the Church in England,' taking cover under the qualifying phrase 'so far as the Law of God allows'. But when Henry broke with Rome and Convocation knuckled under, More resigned his office and withdrew altogether from public office, hoping to stay alive by staying silent. He refused to swear to the Act of Succession and went to prison for his refusal, but so long as he kept silent about his reasons for refusing, he couldn't be condemned as a traitor.

As Bolt put it in September 1960 in his preface to the published script of the play,

> Thomas More, as I wrote about him, became for me a man with an adamantine sense of his own self. He knew where he began and left off, what area of himself he could yield to the encroachments of his enemies, and what to the encroachments of those he loved. It was a substantial area in both cases for he had a proper sense of fear and was a busy lover. Since he was a clever man and a great lawyer he was able to retire from those areas in wonderfully good order, but at length he was asked to retreat from that final area where he located his self.

Robert Bolt

He also apologizes in the preface for 'treating Thomas More, a Christian Saint, as a hero of selfhood'. At one point in the play, he makes 'self' synoynymous in More's eyes with 'soul'.

> MORE: In matters of conscience, the loyal subject is more bounden to be loyal *to* his conscience than to any other thing.
> CROMWELL (*breathing hard: straight at* MORE): – And so provide a noble motive for his frivolous self-conceit!
> MORE (*earnestly*): It is not so, Master Cromwell – very and pure necessity for respect of my own soul.
> CROMWELL: – Your own self you mean!
> MORE: Yes, a man's soul is his self!

At another, the self is equated with the love of God:

> MORE (*gently*): I can't give in, Howard – (*smile*) you might as well advise a man to change the colour of his eyes. I can't. Our friendship's more mutable than *that*.
> NORFOLK: Oh, that's immutable is it? The one fixed point in a world of changing friendships is that Thomas More will not give in!
> MORE (*urgent to explain*): To me it *has* to be, for that's myself! Affection goes as deep in me as you I think, but only God is love right through, Howard; and *that's* my *self*.

In a talk on the BBC Third Programme, Anthony Kenny has argued that these equations are unhistorical and that Bolt's More uses the word 'conscience' in a sense it did not have in the sixteenth century. Taken out of context, many of More's pronouncements can give the impression that he anticipated Kant in holding that the individual must make his own moral decisions, but in their context, they show that More followed Aquinas's doctrine of conscience, seeing it not as an arbiter but as an opinion about God's law. By this reasoning, it's possible to follow your conscience and still be acting immorally, for your conscience can be mistaken. The historical More would never have said:

> What matters to me is not whether it's true or not but that I believe it to be true, or rather not that I *believe* it, but that *I* believe it.

44

Not that Bolt is obliged, any more than Shakespeare was, to make a historical play historically accurate, but he makes his hero inconsistent in condemning Roper as a heretic, for when he became a Lutheran, he was merely acting in accordance with what *he* believed. What's much more important, though, is that in using More to adumbrate an individualism which didn't exist in the sixteenth century, Bolt tends to isolate More from his historical context. This may be part of the reason (conscious or unconscious) for putting More's family relationships so much in the foreground. As in *Flowering Cherry* and *The Tiger and the Horse,* almost all the crucial scenes are played out with the family.

The play opens in More's home with the Common Man setting the scene and interpolating a chorus-type introduction for each of the characters as they come on – Rich, Norfolk, Lady Alice, More's wife, Margaret, their daughter. So, from the beginning, we start to see things through a domestic filter. There can only be a limited amount of interaction between More and his wife and daughter: they can't alter his thinking, which is done when he's alone, and all he can do in the scenes with them is explain conclusions which he's already reached. He's concerned about whether they understand, but he's immune to their efforts to influence his actions, as a weaker man might not be. But certainly they have the power to move him and certainly the relationships between the three of them deepen as the play develops. The basis is laid for this in the first scene when we see the women's anxiety at the summons More receives in the middle of the night to see Wolsey. This prepares the ground for the pressure they are later to put on him to submit to the King's will, and for the growth of a mutual fondness which continues through a conflict in which they can't help continuing the pressure and he can't help continuing his resistance to it.

There are, of course, important scenes which don't involve the family at all. Most of these are concerned with other attempts to put pressure on him, as Henry does himself, as Wolsey and Cromwell both do on Henry's behalf, as Chapuys, the Spanish Ambassador, does on his King's behalf, and as Norfolk does, both in his private role as a friend and in his public role as Chairman of the Commission appointed by the King's Council to inquire into the case of Sir Thomas

Robert Bolt

More. So More's relationships with these characters are partly personality-relationships and partly viewpoint-relationships with the parties, interests and opinions that they represent.

There are also a few scenes in which More doesn't appear: the conspiracy scene between Cromwell and Rich, a short scene these two have with Chapuys, and of course all the Common Man's monologues. But the heart of the play is devoted to More the family man.

The second family scene takes place at three o'clock in the morning – much of the action is at night – when More returns home from Wolsey to find Roper in the house. Roper announces that he's going to be called to the Bar and that he wants to marry Margaret. As a Lutheran, he's not at all an acceptable son-in-law, so this provides a surefire theatrical situation. But once the issues of heresy and the need to reform in the church had been raised, it ought to have paid off theatrically to have explored More's attitude on these points a little more deeply. With only dim memories of sixteenth-century history lessons, most of us bracket More, Colet and Erasmus together as apostles of the New Learning, but what exactly the New Learning was, we no longer know, if we ever did. Of course, in this scene, More's feeling about reform – and about the Reformation – are only relevant in so far as they condition his feelings about Roper. The result is that, as with the arguments about the Bomb in *The Tiger and the Horse*, big issues are effectively reduced in size by making them no more than the subjects of domestic disputes. It's not enough just to dramatize the conflicts between characters who have differing opinions about the big issues when the conflicts between them are centred on their personal relationships.

ROPER: The Church is heretical! Doctor Luther's proved that to my satisfaction!

MORE: Luther's an excommunicate.

ROPER: From a heretic Church! Church? It's a shop — Forgiveness by the florin! Joblots now in Germany!... Mmm, and divorces.

MORE (*expressionless*): Divorces?

ROPER: Oh, half England's buzzing with that.

MORE: 'Half England.' The Inns of Court may be buzzing, England doesn't buzz so easily.

ROPER: It will. And is that a Church? Is that a Cardinal? Is that a Pope? Or Antichrist! (MORE *looks up angrily.* MARGARET *signals frantically.*) Look, what I know I'll say!

MARGARET: You've no sense of the *place*!

MORE (*rueful*): He's no sense of the time.

ROPER: I — (*But* MORE *gently holds up his hand and he stops.*)

MORE: Listen, Roper. Two years ago you were a passionate Churchman; now you're a passionate – Lutheran. We must just pray, that when your head's finished turning your face is to the front again.

This skates over a number of very interesting surfaces and it's not simply a matter of ignoring their dramatic potential. By giving such a cursory glance to the historical context, Bolt is in effect taking his characters out of it. This is why we get so little sense from *A Man for All Seasons* that one age is coming to an end and another beginning. What the play is implicitly saying is that conflicts may be fought out over different ground from one century to another, but that the conflicts and the personalities are themselves essentially the same.

Bolt has swung to a position at the opposite extreme from his earlier Marxism, and he defends the new position theoretically in the preface, which argues that nothing is real except the personality and personal relationships:

'Religion' and 'economy' are abstractions which describe the way men live. Because men work we may speak of an economy, not the other way round. Because men worship we may speak of a religion, not the other way round. And when an economy collides with a religion it is living men who collide, nothing else (they collide with one another and within themselves). Perhaps a few people would disagree with that, put like that, and in theory. But in pratice our theoreticians seem more and more to work the other way round, to derive the worker *from* his economy, the thinker *from* his culture, and we to derive even ourselves from our society and our location in it.

But it isn't as if each individual sits down to make a private decision about whether to worship and whether to work. People worship because they're taught to worship by their parents and get conditioned by schools and churches in which they watch other people worshipping. They work because they're socially conditioned to believe that working is the natural way of spending the time and because our society is organized in such a way that you have to work in order to eat. But other societies have differed and the 'work' done by an eleventh-century Egyptian slave or a six-teenth-century English peasant were so different from that done by a twentieth-century factory worker that it's almost begging the question to describe them all by the same word 'work'. Obviously our sense of identity and our behaviour in our personal relationships depends very largely on which period and which society we're born into – and whereabouts within it.

By concentrating on personal relationships and thinning down the social texture, Bolt tends to make all his sixteenth-century characters modern. Of course he's perfectly entitled to be less interested in how sixteenth-century people differed from us than in how they resembled us and he uses the figure of the Common Man quite deliberately to embody 'that which is common to us all'. He doesn't always avoid modernisms in the Common Man's speeches to the audience and by making him quote from history books about More, he makes him seem to be standing outside history. So when he dons costumes to play all the working-class parts in the play – steward, boatman, jailer, executioner – this has the effect of zooming us in and out of the histori-cal picture. Certainly this serves a useful purpose in underlining the similarities between non-heroic, vulgar, venal, insensitive behaviour then and non-heroic, vulgar, venal, insensitive behaviour now, but it might have been better if the moralist in Bolt had joined forces with the historian.

Like the 'Epic' division of the play into more or less self-contained scenes and like the use of titles and props flown down from the flies, the use of the Common Man is one of the devices in the play which owe their origin to Brecht. Bolt said in the preface:

> The style I eventually used was a bastardized version of the one most recently associated with Bertolt Brecht.

Brecht's alienation effects are aimed primarily at preventing his audience from identifying emotionally with his characters. Bolt's purposes are diametrically opposite. The Common Man 'is intended to draw the audience into the play, not thrust them off it'.

Although any playwright is at perfect liberty to borrow Brechtian stylistic devices without wanting to focus his subject-matter in the same way as Brecht, it may be dangerous to, because they are, above all, focusing devices. The Common Man is given excellent lines for striking up a friendly relationship with the audience and Leo McKern both had fun himself and gave us fun, but the main picture got blurred in two ways. The polarity between More and the Common Man would have been more dramatically profitable if one of them had been distinctively a man of his period and the other more modern. But in different ways, both get abstracted from history. As chorus, the Common Man never sinks fully into any of his roles, and More is modern in his individualism.

What also occurs is a blurring of the social background through the use of the Common Man to play so many roles, amusing though this is. Like Brecht's Galileo, More is a hero who withdraws into silence to avoid martyrdom. Both get completely isolated from contemporary society, but Galileo's isolation is more theatrically effective because we see exactly what it is that he's isolated from. Brecht builds up a great many social elements very solidly – men in the street, monks, cardinals, a landlady, soldiers, burghers, academics and the Papal court. In sketching all this in, Brecht wasn't just creating historical atmosphere or touching in a colourful background, he was enriching his dramatic field of play. The people with whom Galileo collides are seen both as individuals and as representatives of groups, indexes to the social, political, religious and economic pressures that have conditioned them. More's isolation could also have been presented as a relationship – and not an altogether negative one – with the whole of contemporary society.

I think it's a great pity that Bolt decided not to develop the relationship with Henry beyond the one scene. It's an excellent scene. Henry's abrupt shifts of mood and changes of subject characterize him very well and we get a good impression of a mutual admiration between the two men that counterpoints the head-on clash. The advantage of using the King himself in a historical play, as Shakespeare so often found, is that the one man symbolizes the whole country. Henry VIII *was* England then as nobody is England today. It's true that Cromwell's underhand methods and Rich's greedy

Robert Bolt

corruptibility also convey a good deal about the way these affairs were handled, but in More's scenes with them, the personal relationships are nothing like so integral to the clash of viewpoint and interest as with Henry, and More's only other fully three-dimensional relationships are with the family.

The third family scene is the one which frames the scene with Henry. Before the meeting, Alice is put out by More's failure to dress better for the occasion; after it her anxiety provokes one of his statements about the self.

> ALICE: Be ruled! If you won't rule him, be ruled!
> MORE (*quietly*): I neither could nor would rule my King. (*Pleasantly.*) But there's a little ... little, area ... where I must rule myself. It's very little – less to him than a tennis court. (*Her face is still full of foreboding: he sighs.*)

And when Rich appears, ostensibly to warn More against Cromwell and Chapuys, and to denounce the steward for passing information to them, both Alice and Margaret warn More that Rich himself is spying on him. But More is stoical and indifferent. In any case he says there's nothing he can do.

The first family scene in Act Two is the one in which he resigns his office as Chancellor. Bolt involves Alice and Margaret even in the gesture by which he signals his resignation, when he asks for help in taking the chain off his neck. Alice refuses; Roper, now married to Margaret, offers to help but it's only from Margaret that More will accept help. And when Alice asks about his future, he describes the private life that he hopes to lead.

> ALICE: So there's an end of you. What will you do now – sit by the fire and make goslings in the ash?
> MORE: Not at all, Alice, I expect I'll write a bit. (*He woos them with unhappy cheerfulness.*) I'll write, I'll read, I'll think. I think I'll learn to fish! I'll play with my grandchildren – when son Roper's done his duty. (*Eager.*) Alice, shall I teach you to read?
> ALICE: No, by God!

The second is the scene in which Margaret comes in carrying a bundle of bracken. They burn it to keep warm and live on a diet of stinking mutton and parsnips. Alice complains and her disaffection works as a foil for More's resignation and cheerfulness under duress.

Margaret is a witness of the quarrel that More fabricates with Norfolk to free him from the burden of friendship, and with Roper, she brings her father news of the new oath that has to be sworn to the Act of Succession. But though their only active function in this scene is as messengers, Roper's truculence provides the pretext and they both provide the audience for one of More's best speeches:

> MORE: Let's get home. (*He turns and sees* ROPER *excited and truculent.*) Now listen, Will. And, Meg, you know I know you well, you listen too. God made the *angels* to show him splendour – as he made animals for innocence and plants for their simplicity. But Man he made to serve him wittily, in the tangle of his mind! If he suffers us to fall to such a case that there is no escaping, then we may stand to our tackle as best we can, and yes, Will, then we may clamour like champions . . . if we have the spittle for it. And no doubt it delights God to see splendour where he only looked for complexity. But it's God's part, not our own, to bring ourselves to that extremity! Our natural business lies in escaping – so let's get home and study this Bill.

The final and most important family scene of all comes when they visit him in prison. Alice has aged and Margaret is now under oath to try to persuade her father to swear to the Act. This is theatrically the best of the family scenes, not just because of the situation but partly because the fact of domesticity is itself put into focus by the very anomaly of speaking about custard and dresses when this may be the last time they'll ever see each other. Bolt deliberately makes More's behaviour inconsistent. At one moment he's limiting himself to saying what a delicious custard it is and what a nice dress; at the next he's saying that he doesn't see how he can face death unless Alice will tell him that she understands.

And to Margaret he explains why he can't take the oath:

> When a man takes an oath, Meg, he's holding his own self in his own hands. Like water (*cups hands*) and if he opens his fingers *then* – he needn't hope to find himself again. Some men aren't

capable of this, but I'd be loathe to think your father one of them.

Like the characters, the language straddles the sixteenth century and the twentieth. It was puzzling that so many critics failed to detect the amount of quotation that Bolt had incorporated into his text. Many of More's speeches, like the 'God made the angels ...' speech, are liberally peppered with cadences that have an unmistakable sixteenth-century ring to them and, as Anthony Kenny pointed out, his final speech to the court is made up mainly of verbatim quotations from Harpesfield's Life. But many of the quotations are slightly adapted, reducing the discrepancy between More's prose and Bolt's, which aims, successfully, at neutrality, avoiding modernism without attempting pastiche. Though there are some passages where the rhythm and syntax is so typically sixteenth-century that they do contrast noticeably with the smoother modern cadences of most of the writing. For instance when More is accosted on the scaffold by Catherine Anger, the woman who tried to bribe him with the silver cup that he gave away to Rich:

> You have no injury; so go your ways; and content yourself; and trouble me not!

This is based on a different syntax from

> Oh, it's only a life-line, we shan't have to use it but it's comforting to have. No, no, when they find I'm silent they'll ask nothing better than to leave me silent; you'll see.

But all in all, the neutrality and the straddling work triumphantly.

The conscious use of imagery is more questionable. As Bolt said in his *Encore* interview, 'There are about 120 images of the sea, of fishing, of navigation and so on, in *A Man for All Seasons*, which have a very specific purpose.' The purpose is described in the preface:

> As a figure for the superhuman context I took the largest, most alien, least formulated thing I know, the sea and water. The references to ships, rivers, currents, tides, navigation, and so on, are all used for this purpose. Society by contrast figures as dry land.

I doubt whether this kind of planning bears any useful fruits; on the other hand the sheer abundance of images does help Bolt's prose to fit in with the quotations.

> MORE (*roused and excited*): Oh? (*Advances on* ROPER.) And when the last law was down, and the Devil turned round on you – where would you hide, Roper, the laws all being flat? (*Leaves him.*) This country's planted thick with laws from coast to coast – Man's laws, not God's – and if you cut them down – and you're just the man to do it – d'you really think you could stand upright in the winds that would blow then? (*Quietly.*) Yes, I'd give the Devil benefit of law, for my own safety's sake.

I don't know whether there's any actual quotation from More in this passage. The phrases 'and you're just the man to do it' and 'd'you really think you could' look very modern, isolated from their context, but heard in their context, they're quite acceptable because the dense imagery of the preceding few lines and the rhythm that they create are still echoing in our ears. And this is typical of the play. The problem of language in a historical play is always a delicate one and to have come as close as this to solving it is a very impressive feat.

GENTLE JACK

Gentle Jack was produced at the Queen's Theatre in November 1963 with Dame Edith Evans and Kenneth Williams in a production by Noel Willman, who directed *A Man for All Seasons,* but it only ran for seventy-five performances until the beginning of February. Audiences were both confused and hostile: Bolt himself has described their reactions in an interview:*

> Normally when they don't like a play, they cough. It's as simple as that, and by having some mechanical device for registering sound in the auditorium you could draw a graph of interest and un-interest: but in this play they sat like mice, in a chilled, dead silence that vibrated with hostility, except for occasional yelps of laughter from here and there which the actors found very unnerving. They didn't know what was happening in the auditorium and neither did I. It was quite spooky.

Nevertheless, it's one of Bolt's most interesting pieces of writing, certainly his most original, not only in structure and style, but also in substance, though it's not difficult to see why the play failed to ignite theatrically. It's an adult fairy-tale with a modern setting. It tries to encompass both fantasy and satire with a complicated plot that involves several shifts between two subjects and two areas of action.

The two killings which end the play inevitably challenge comparison with the ritual murder in David Rudkin's *Afore Night Come,* but it can't generate the same theatrical excitement when the hero is killed because the rustic workmen who kill him haven't acquired the same three-dimensionality. They are very minor characters, and except for Jacko, who is common to both halves of the plot, even the major characters suffer from the way that the play cuts from one half to the other.

The first scene in Violet Lazara's office suggests that this female Lazarus will be developed in some depth. As Bolt described it in

*Theatre at Work, edited by Charles Marowitz and Simon Trussler. Methuen.

John Normington (left) as Sir Oblong and Davyd Harries as Obidiah in the Aldwych production of *The Thwarting of Baron Bolligrew*

Paul Scofield and Andrew Keir as Thomas More and Thomas Cromwell
in *A Man for All Seasons* at the Globe Theatre

the interview, the concept of her character is a very interesting one:

> She was a woman who had achieved enormous, barren wealth, who was, late in life, although still beautiful, a virgin, childless, and who, above all, lived by figures which are the *ne plus ultra* of abstraction.

But the theatrical possibilities of this aren't explored. The first scene in the office establishes the characters who work for her, and her relationships with them. Champion, the Director of Accounts, serves as a chorus to introduce the play, as the Common Man did, but, as he describes them, Violet's business affairs sound every bit as boring as Cherry's insurance office.

> CHAMPION: My name is Champion and I am as it were Chief Secretary of State to a considerable Empire. I am Miss Violet Lazara's Director of Accounts. Our assets in round figures are – (*he recites just too fast to follow*) twenty-five millions of real estate, twelve and a half million gilt-edged stock, nineteen million industrials, nine millions in municipal bonds mostly South American. Please keep count. I am reducing rupees, roubles, lira, dollars, deutschmark, yen, to pounds for your convenience – five millions in short-term loans. We are controlling interests in Trading Trusts with Active Assets of say thirty millions and a half. The total, for anybody slow, is one hundred and one millions.

Probably, too, it's bad tactics to give the audience something they can't follow right at the outset.

Of the young men working for Violet, Bilbo Cubitt is her favourite. He's handsome, well-groomed and clever, while Jacko Cadence, who is clumsy, humble, hard-working and spectacled, irritates her with his every effort to please her, and with every squeak of his boots. Much of the opening scene is given over to the baiting of Jacko and to the contrast between the two young men, while also laying the foundations for an unrealistic style. Stage directions describe the disciplined barking laugh in which the characters all join, and the device of freezing them into groups and then animating them again. The stage business through which Violet's activities are established is itself unrealistic, though less clearly stylized. Both Bilbo and Violet address the audience directly. There's no clear differentiation between their styles of speaking. Both use clean-cut, short sentences, but neither speak colloquially.

BILBO : Twenty years ago I suppose she was 'a fascinating bitch'; now she's less fascinating. Yes, I know. (*He is not sharing a joke with them, but coldly correcting them for a vulgar error.*) She's rich, though. And our noses, tongues and other appendages are not more personal than our balance in the bank. Ask anybody poor. She's not uncomely. Beautifully clean. And rich. It's my belief that opulence unclothed even might be exciting; might be magnificent.

(BILBO *exits down* L. VIOLET *turns and addresses the audience.*)

VIOLET : He'll catch the plane tonight; tomorrow night he will be – where? The bullfight? Hardly. But wherever, he'll be there because I sent him; I've won again. But a woman who wins, who always wins, is that a woman? (*She contemplates her own body.*) Oh, yes, that's a woman. And an old one. With not much time to learn the posture of defeat. And that time bought with money. Good grief, my body knows the trick already – merely sleep defeats my body every night. But to make my *mind* fall backwards ... He'll be naked somewhere – in some room – in some garden – under trees – some music playing – or whatever else it is they do. And I'll be at my country 'property', well-clothed, very well-clothed. (*To Jacko; with startling venom.*) With you, you pitiable thing!

The body-mind distinction is typical of the tendency to divide things into opposites and the opposition between nakedness and having clothes on prefigures the 'unbutton' motif, with which the sexy Lady Penelope is later to assault Jacko, and of course clothes suggest the opposite of Pan's mode of being.

The transition from the office set to the garden of Attis Hall is effected without a break in continuity. Foliage is flown in, together with a large picture of the hall in the middle distance, which replaces the office window, and four country servants carry on rustic furniture while a secretary and three clerks carry off the office furniture. Jacko stays on stage thoughout the transition, which is covered by 'music of the insects'. Then the new scene starts with a new character, Dr

Morgan, who describes himself in his speech to the audience as Violet's Court Philosopher. His conversation with Jacko fills us in on the background to this part of the plot. Violet now owns the estate which used to belong to Jacko's father, and because the old man died, presumably of grief, she now feels so guilty that she wants to give it back to Jacko, who has a long speech explaining his reasons for not wanting it.

> JACKO: And I hate every leaf. And every insect. I hate the smell of leaves and the sound of insects. When I was a little boy, once I dug a grave in the forest, for my father, which I told him was a bear-trap. When I told him that he thought I'd got the right idea and I had a gamekeeper to help me. The soil there's very soft. Leaf mould. Dead leaves, dead fruits, anything dead, corrupted into soil by worms that live in it and won't take 'no' for an answer. It's centuries deep and, naturally, fertile. If I were Violet I'd have scooped it up with machines and sold. I hate every item in the schedule; mists and muck, hard horn, wet orifice, the skyline and greasy pail, dung, hung game, cattle giving birth and being killed, the workers and their wives, sharp knives, stags, stallions, the whole extreme rude cruel way my father lived. But most of all I hate those trees that stand there. Do you know he could have saved himself by cutting down those trees.

Intrinsically the imagery in this prose is quite rich and ranges over a wide area of experience, but the organization of it in the speech doesn't altogether succeed in developing it. It sounds too much like a catalogue of items that Jacko hates. Instead of being linked together in a way that produces some sort of organic growth, the images stay separate, like beads on a string.

Before we meet Lady Penelope, we hear that she's 'picking flowers for the King' and it's only later that it becomes clear this is the garland for the 'King' who is to be elected as part of the pagan rite which is observed here each year. This now becomes central to the action. It would be very difficult for a play to unite this world with the world of the office, especially with only tenuous support from a plot in which Jacko is the only strong link between the two halves. Violet figures in the Attis Abbey action, but only peripherally.

Robert Bolt

The problem of finding the right focus is further complicated by the introduction of a bevy of minor characters, who have problems which are later to be resolved by Jacko when the god endows him with Panic powers. Rev. Treadgold, the man who has kept the pagan ceremony alive, acts as guide to the others, which enables him to explain to us a good deal about the history of Attis Abbey and its traditional association with the god Pan – or 'Jack-in-the-Green', an English variant of his name. Gaston Dupont is an attractive young Frenchman. Lady Cynthia Dalrymple is his rich, spoilt, immature girl-friend, who hasn't yet slept with him. Mr and Mrs Bracket are a childless married couple in their forties who wander around holding hands but secretly detest each other. Their problem is whether to divorce.

As types, these are all rather too well defined. Bolt has, to a very limited extent, identified with Jacko, but these are all very much 'characters' and their tendency to comment on themselves from outside only emphasizes the fact. 'All virgins are smutty,' Cynthia says apologetically to Penelope. Penelope, a major character, tries to see herself from inside and from outside at the same time:

> I wish, I wish I was a virgin. My word, I'd notice. I'd notice the first time. (*She humbly corrects herself.*) I'd try. I always try. I tried the second time. And the third time, and the fourth and forty-fourth time. And I tried the five hundred and sixty-seventh time, last Sunday morning, with Samuel Simms in Billy Bowker's loft. Or was it Billy in Samuel's loft? The only difference I can notice is the number. I've got better at it, certainly. Got good at it. Had some good teachers. And I think I may say I have a natural flair for it. I'm of an inventive turn of body. I am. I am not a nice young woman. That makes no difference, either. Practice makes practised, that's all that practice makes. The only time that's different is the first time because that's where you begin. And presumably the last time because that's where you leave off. But you don't know which the last time is. It might be something, if you did. Condemned men eat hearty breakfasts. Yes, if you could know the last time – but *know* – if you had taken in, digested and excreted *that* – your appetites might put our branches, leaves and flowers, your birds might sing, rivers run, and

all your faculties, notice. My word, you'd need to know, though.

Certainly this is writing which makes a serious effort to penetrate beneath the surface behaviour and to get away from conventional types. Comparing this with the dialogue in *Flowering Cherry* and *The Tiger and the Horse*, it's not just a difference of style or focus, it's a basic difference in subject matter. Penelope is less commonplace and more interesting, as well as being less realistic. She is partly a humour, as in a Ben Jonson play, partly a Vice as in a medieval morality. Possibly the drive of her energies is oversimplified theatrically, particularly in the scene where she pursues Jacko with a pair of scissors, determined to cut off all the buttons from his clothes, but if she's a failure, she's a thoroughly worthwhile one. The simplification could have worked if the whole play had stuck to this fairy-tale level, but it doesn't.

Perhaps the basic failure is due to what is really an attempt to integrate two separate plays into one. The only connection between Violet and Pan is her total denial of him, and though this could have been quite enough, had it been developed, her mere presence in the country and her position as the owner of the estate and Jacko's employer isn't nearly enough to relate her to the Panic part of the action. When she arrives at Attis Hall with her retinue, the conversation turns immediately to Bilbo and her Mexican hotels. He has sold them for her without a specific briefing, so she has ordered him to buy them back, but it turns out to be an extraordinarily expensive operation. When Jacko appears, she joins with the others in baiting him, and the conversation turns to clothes again:

VIOLET: I appeal to you. Could anything look less Squirearchal?
CHAMPION: No, a thorough-going City man is Mr Cadence.
VIOLET: Stuff. The way he wears a City suit's the only rustic thing about him.
(*All are amused. Even* HUBERT, *aware that Jacko is in some way being baited, guffaws and slaps his knee.*)
Remember, Hubert, if a City man can't wear a City suit he can't do anything. It's his only function.

But Jacko isn't important enough to her scenes and she's almost irrelevant to his. It's the country servants who provoke him into an explicit statement of his difficulties in directing aggression outwards:

> It seems that Nature's made me inside out and all my outer parts like fists and teeth are cramped in here – (*he indicates his stomach*) and all that uncouth stuff which should be left in darkness, is exhibited, in me.

Soon – but it's already rather late in the play – it becomes clear that Jacko is to be elected 'King' and that this will now be our main concern. And right at the end of the first of the two acts, after he's been provoked into lashing out at Hubert, a sort of village idiot, and after blood has been spilled, Jack-in-the-Green appears in person, a divine *alter ego* for Jacko.

> *He is of no age; a pandering urchin, infinitely irresponsible; a fallen god, suffering and withdrawn. A liar and a teacher, a murderer and a benefactor, he is finally impersonal, like a cold wind. His charm is absolute, but to himself all human contact is an ignoble imposition and painful charade.*

He demonstrates his divine powers by 'felling' Jacko with a drum thump and a cymbal clash when he tries to run away, clicking his fingers to make fruit fall out of the flies, conjuring music from nowhere and causing snow to fall. But before anything else can happen, the act is over.

At the beginning of Act Two, he performs a different sort of stage conjuring trick with the carcass of Penelope's dog, which he has killed:

> *With the triumphant air of a conjurer,* JACK *spins it aloft. Its under-belly gapes open and a mess of glistening entrails hangs out.* JACKO *rises and recoils galvanically, pointing, horrified.*

His main weapon, though, is persuasion, but the language doesn't always rise to the occasion:

> Now, listen. If you want, you can go. You can go, and tell yourself you 'met an "incubus", a "goblin", "boggart", "sprite", "demon", "devil", "imp", "elf", "troll", "hallucination".' Ha! You 'were "bewitched", "possessed", "enchanted", "had a nervous breakdown".' In the Forest. If you want. But you'll have had your one chance – Jacko. Isn't that the truth? How-

ever, if you want ... (*He turns away on this seemingly in-different.*)

(JACKO *finds he can move and turns to go.*)

(*He turns and yells, malignant and pathetic*) Go on!
     Back to your sadness and your resignation and seduction, and
     your unlived life – that's beginning to stink on you – d'you
     know that? Go on! Back to your avoided days. Your abstract
     hours, your millions of disembodied minutes. And your heavy
     dreams – that are destroying you – d'you know that? *(Be-seeching.)* Or stay, and let me help you. There is a place for you
     in Nature. How could there not be? You have no other place.

Like Jacko's speech about the Attis Hall estate, this is too much like a
prosaic catalogue to achieve its purpose in characterizing the god.
Although pleasantly remote from conventional Pans, he talks too
much like a psychiatrist and not sufficiently like a god.

Then, when Penelope appears, he has some fun with a game Ariel
played in *The Tempest*, making himself invisible and speaking, so that
she thinks it's Jacko's voice she's hearing. The game encourages
Jacko to imitate Jack's audacity and this pays immediate dividends
in altering her attitude to him.

PENELOPE: Jacko ... ?
JACKO (*turning to her*): You still here?
PENELOPE: What's happened to you, Jacko?
JACKO: I've been 'unbuttoned' —
JACK: – darling.

This is amusing, and clear, but some of Jack's speeches are both
difficult to follow and unhelpful in demonstrating what he stands for:

     Dogs – they move by the fire and fart – that's humble. But their
     eyes shine, Jacko.
JACKO: Dogs —
JACK: – fight. Yes, I know. Terribly, considering their size; that
     terrible anxiety dogs fight with. But a dog with its teeth in
     another dog's throat is not so terrible as a man in an office; and
     everyone knows this. And dogs are half-corrupted, dogs are
     tame – a lion, now – what a machine! What a voice! Dignity!
     Mine, too. Let's face it, dear, you have lacked dignity. But

Robert Bolt

with a box of matches – (*he rises, crosses to Jacko and puts the blossom in Jacko's jacket*) any man can make a lion tremble. (*He sniggers.*) It's true – matches – dry sticks – fire; he slams his tail between his legs and soils himself. (*The snigger vanishes.*) And in that moment, cringing and collapsed – he has more, oh, much, a world more dignity, than the split, harsh thing that lit the fire and doesn't know itself. All growth and strength. Oak beams hold up stone towers for generations. And who was ever hurt by the growing of an oak? (*As he says this he spreads his hands as one who has nothing to hide, and they are crimson from his handling of the dog. He smiles foolishly and wipes them together.*)

However, he enters into an arrangement with Jacko which seems quite clear. Jacko can borrow the divine powers for one week – so long as he stays in the forest. If he goes back into the house, the contract is terminated without notice. Most of the rest of the play is concerned with the use he makes of the powers. To begin with, he starts to talk very differently. When he hears that Violet has told Cynthia that disposing of her virginity is a bargain she can only make once and that she should therefore hold out for the best possible terms, this is how he reacts:

> It cannot have escaped your notice Cynthia, that this 'bargain' is a bargain which Miss Lazara has so far been unable to negotiate for herself. Wisdom prevents; I recommend folly. Wisdom is knowledge and knowledge is power and Miss Lazara's powerful. But power is possession and having and being are separate modes; knowing and doing are separate modes. So, Cynthia, will you have your life or live it? Will you *do* what you want or will you, like Miss Lazara, be self-possessed?

This is an oddly academic and literary way for Jacko to talk now that he's under the Panic influence.

But he goes on to be more commonsensical and he's effective in persuading the lovers who have held back for so long to get into bed together.

> I'm saying, Cynthia, that since you began to count your days

you haven't been a child. I'm right about that, am I? The clock has started?

CYNTHIA: Yes.

JACKO: Tick tock. If you count them you must live them. Life won't live them for you any more. Tick tock in any case. *Do*, darling, or you're playing leapfrog with a skeleton. Not now, too late; back over back; out of youth, through middle-age to ugliness; and one day – plop – too late; the girl's gone; the skeleton stands upright, and the earth starts sliding.

Some of the images and figures of speech may be whimsical, but at least the sense is clear.

The Brackets get told that they don't even like each other and there's a very amusing scene when Jacko proves his point, demonstrating the extent of their mutual irritation. The dialogue bursts delightfully into a celebration of dislike as the long suppressed complaints fly out into the open:

MRS BRACKET: You don't wash your hands. You eat like a dog. You've got varicose veins.

BRACKET: You talk to yourself.

MRS BRACKET: You're dull.

BRACKET: You're unhappy.

MRS BRACKET: You're lazy in bed.

BRACKET: I'm bored in bed.

MRS BRACKET: It's all that hot milk.

BRACKET: It's those interlock nighties.

MRS BRACKET: You're one of the boys. You miss your mother. You only know two jokes, and they're both about the RAF.

BRACKET: Joy, Joy —

MRS BRACKET: Yes?

BRACKET: – I've read your diary.

MRS BRACKET: Stirling!

BRACKET: Joy!

(They run together and clasp hands.)

You don't like me.

MRS BRACKET *(radiant)*: I hate you!

BRACKET *(radiant)*: I hate you, too!

Robert Bolt

And Jacko ceremonially separates them.

He enjoys his new freedom and his new strength, but though Jack had promised that he could borrow free of interest and without any obligation, it turns out that he has to pay very heavily.

> JACK: You borrowed me. (*Gravely and warningly.*) Not just a bit of me – so far and no farther – all of me. *Do* you want me?
> JACKO: Yes.
> JACK: Then you want what I want. (*He moves to Jacko.*) You know what I want. (*He slips the knife into Jacko's hand. Coaxingly.*) Don't you?

And when Jacko demurs at killing, Jack gets furious with him for thinking he can have it both ways. Someone must be killed. There has to be blood.

> What do they think I am – a relaxation? Do they think that they can call me, and rouse me, and torment me – and then – send me back? Do they think I am – a holiday? (*He rises.*) Oh, very well, very well. I must fend for myself. (*He goes on to the right end of the lower rostrum.*) We'll do it the old way. I will fend for myself. (*He turns to go but is arrested by a thought.*) Unless . . . (*He moves down R and offers the knife, haft first, to the audience.*) Is there an animal in the House? Someone who will stand up for what he wants – a natural man? I am your nature, and I want it. (*He crosses down L.*) You, sir? You would be under my protection – I am a god. I am a very great god. No? All – thoughtful? *(He moves down C.)* Lot of little Platos, are we? (*Sadly.*) There was a time . . . (*He hears his own phrase. A last hope dawns. Eagerly.*) There was a time, when meadow, grove and stream, the earth, and every common sight, to you did seem apparelled in celestial light, the glory and the freshness of a dream. Remember?

We also find out that the minor characters aren't satisfied with the solutions that Jacko has found for them. Mrs Bracket is still set on the divorce but Mr Bracket is having second thoughts. Gaston and Cynthia have slept together, but she says she didn't feel a thing. He has taken something from her and given her nothing in return, and she accuses him of not looking naked when his clothes are off.

The man Jack kills is Dr Morgan, who has never been much more than a *raisonneur,* never been properly integrated in the action. But first he has a long speech which is rather reminiscent of Whiting's *A Penny for a Song,* though it's more explicit:

> You think because I am a man of mind I cannot know the nature of your suffering. That's wrong. Because I am, I do. For you are like me, Jacko – *me.* Except that you're a fool. You've sided with the body, with simple, baying matter, and you hope for happiness. Attend to me. Matter scrutinized by mind becomes a sort of whirling grit, is it not so? In which what you would call a man is momentary complexity, only well expressed in figures. One, two, three, four, five, six, seven, eight, nine and nought. That's the Life of Nature and compared with that, Death's rowdy. And this knowledge is what mind is. And mind is all that man is. There are not many men. Accept. Be quiet. And be one. Oh, arrogate no special fitness to yourself because you call your figure 'love'. I know your 'love' is a figure.

And Jack, who had previously seemed to need a human to do the killing for him, plunges the knife in, so that Jacko will be blamed and killed.

This is how Bolt (in the interview in *Theatre at Work*) summed up what the god stands for:

> He says that if you want the rush of spontaneous physical tenderness and emotional fulfilment, with it, as a necessary concomitant, goes the rush of aggression and physical destruction, and he is simply bewildered when the boy, who is meant to embody the central human situation, thinks that he can borrow from the god tenderness and spontaneity, but can deny the god his outbreak of violence.

But naturally the boy would think that, since there was no mention of any condition when the god struck the bargain with him. Possibly we're meant to see him as having wilfully misled Jacko and possibly his behaviour is made to seem unreasonable simply because a god doesn't need to be governed by reason, as we see it. But the play confuses because it doesn't succeed in focusing the unreasonableness.

Robert Bolt

I have no doubt though that in writing about the polarity between gentleness and destructiveness, Bolt has found a theme which is capable of involving him far more deeply as a writer than any of his previous themes. The very fact that he's failed to master his material this time is promising, for it's arguable that his earlier plays exercised too complete a mastery over their material, and it's good news that he now intends to have another go at the theme of *Gentle Jack*.

THE THWARTING OF BARON BOLLIGREW

The Thwarting of Baron Bolligrew is one of the best plays for children which has ever been written. It was first produced by the Royal Shakespeare Company at the Aldwych in December 1965 and revived as a Christmas show in 1966. This was when I saw it and the two children I took (a boy of nine and a girl of eight) both enjoyed it very much. But they were both slightly bothered by the story-teller. They didn't mind his linking narrative between the episodes, but they didn't like it when he got into conversation with the characters.

They are very appealing characters, especially the short, plump, elderly hero. He has a strong moral sense, as we see in the opening scene when the Knights are bringing back the tips from tails of the dragons they've killed and putting them down on the round table in front of the Duke. Now that they've killed off all the dragons in the Dukedom, they feel like taking it easy, but our hero, Sir Oblong Fitz Oblong reminds them of their duties to other areas:

> OBLONG : Now we can move on somewhere else.
> DUKE (*faintly*): . . . Er, 'move on', Oblong?
> OBLONG : Yes, Your Grace.
> DUKE : Whatever for?
> OBLONG (*mildly puzzled*): To succour the poor and needy, Your
>   Grace. Up north, for instance – dragons, barons, goblins.
>   Having a very thin time of it up north, the poor and needy.
> DUKE : But my dear fellow – the climate!
> OBLONG : Well, south, then, Your Grace.

This easy shifting of geographical ground gives us the first hint that there may be something wrong with Oblong's moral sense and as the play goes on, it shows that, like some children, he tries too hard to be good. The modern chatty manner has great charm and Bolt gets the best of both worlds in making the Duke and the Knights like children in their enjoyment of musical bumps, lemonade and ice cream and like adults in the way they combine friendliness with phoneyness when they're trying to get their own way through moral cheating.

> Earned a breather. Well said, Smoothe, Late lie-in in the morning. Bit of jousting in the afternoon perhaps. Substantial supper; jolly good game of musical bumps and off to bed. (*Appealing all round.*) Where's the harm in that?
>
> (*Murmur of considered agreement.*)
>
> I'll put it to the vote. Democratic procedure – Can't say fairer than that, Oblong. All those in favour of the programme just outlined, please say 'Aye'.

We are later to hear much the same tones of sweet reasonableness from the villainous Bolligrew and the children will again be reminded of the methods adults often adopt to take them in.

Oblong's sense of duty is liable to make life less comfortable for the others, so they conspire to get rid of him to the Bolligrew islands. And it isn't difficult to make him go. Outraged to hear that the Baron hunts, and tempted by the chance of becoming a Royal Knight Errant, he accepts the mission. The story-teller announces his appointment and tells us that the brown paper parcel which is thrown on from the wings comes from the King's Court. He unwraps it, takes out a purple robe and helps Oblong on with it. A sea-captain comes on carrying a mast and sail and the two men make their unrealistic voyage through lightning and thunder to the Bolligrew Islands.

Bolligrew's villainy is quickly and amusingly demonstrated. We've heard from the Captain that all he cares about is hunting and grinding the faces of the poor, and he produces a solid gold watch presented to the Master of the Bolligrew Hounds (himself) by the Chairman of the Hunt Committee (himself) and paid for by evicting three or four entire families. We also meet his villainous, saturnine, moustache-chewing henchman, Squire Blackheart, who does most of the evicting work. The children who are too young to know what 'evict' means can appreciate the visual gag which follows immediately when Oblong 'accidentally' steps on Bolligrew's toe in order to make him miss when he takes a pot-shot at a passing magpie.

After searching among his armour for his instructions, and putting on his spectacles to read them, Oblong announces his three objectives: to rebuild the island's church, to restore justice to its magistrate's court and to suppress the dragon. Bolligrew obligingly calls an immediate session of the court by blowing a whistle and presides very funnily and very unfairly, with Blackheart on the bench beside him. The most glaring example of malpractice is the case of Obidiah Bobble-nob, an impecunious egg-painter who has been accused of chucking a brick through one of Bolligrew's greenhouses and keeps getting a pound added on to his fine when he's prevented from paying it by a mysterious hooligan who smashes all his eggs before market-day.

When Bolligrew incites Blackheart to challenge Oblong to a duel, he at first refuses to fight, but he finds that this is losing him the confidence of the villagers, whose help he needs, if he's to rebuild the church. So, much as he'd have preferred to fight violence without using violence, he finds he can't. Screwing himself up to the decision to fight Blackheart, he involves the audience, pantomime fashion, encouraging them to voice their approval.

A conversation with the magpie whose life he saved by stepping on the Baron's toe turns into a moral discussion. We see Oblong at his stuffiest and Mike the Magpie is highly endearing as he promises not to steal any more, and reluctantly joins Oblong in helping Obidiah to paint his eggs before tomorrow's market. Oblong asks the story-teller to bring the moon up so that they can start work and there's another pleasant departure from realism when Blackheart goes out for his midnight walk, preceded by his dog, which is a cut-out on wheels.

The plot lines start to converge when it becomes clear that the Baron's persecution of Obidiah is aimed at getting possession of his cottage and his pond, which is full of trout. And the narrative strands are drawn neatly together when Oblong secures Blackheart's dismissal from the bench by proving that it was he who was smashing Obidiah's eggs. And there is dramatic conflict, too, at each point of the story's progress. Here the Lord Mayor, who is appointed to fill the empty place on the Bench, is chary of sitting, till the Baron has made it quite plain that he wants him to, and even then, it's not at first certain whether he'll have the courage to side with Oblong when he demands that Obidiah's £10 fine should be returned. But again justice prevails.

There are two incidents which combine to provide a good curtain for Act One and to create suspense for Act Two. Bolligrew dictates a letter to Dr Beelzebub Moloch, Dean of the Faculty of Magic and Regius Professor of Wickedness at the University, asking him to come to the island, and a smoking letter arrives from the dragon in an asbestos envelope. It's to say that he's hungry.

We meet Moloch at the beginning of Act Two. He's plotting with Bolligrew against Oblong and against the dragon and he evolves a neat plan to treat the troublesome Knight Errant with a reliable dragon poison and feed him to the beast. To get Oblong to go to the dragon's cave, he will have to be put under a spell. The story-teller is used here – as the Common Man is in *A Man for All Seasons* – both to relieve tension and to screw it up tighter for the next episode. He asks Moloch whether he really wants what's going to happen – which makes it sound as though it's going to be particularly unpleasant.

With his familiar, Mazeppa, another magpie, Moloch prepares the spell. But each time the plot is in need of it, a new obstacle is found to produce dramatic conflict, and now the spell requires Moloch to get hold of a prized possession of Oblong's. His only prized possession is the purple cloak. So how is he to be persuaded to part with it? Moloch's pose as a Professor of Goodness and Bolligrew's spiritual adviser has the incidental effect of satirizing clerical affectations, and it enables him to persuade Oblong that it's vanity never to take the cloak off. He also offers Oblong an apple which, when he eats it, will make him poisonous to dragons.

Again the threads are nicely pulled together when Oblong refuses to listen to Mike's warning about Moloch, even telling the magpie off for maligning the worthy old gentleman. The magic ritual scenes, which are just faintly reminiscent of the pagan ritual which summons the god in *Gentle Jack*, are good theatrical value as spectacle, with explosions, clouds of smoke, magnesium streamers and bashings and twangings of cymbals and harps. While some of the verbal jokes may be fully comprehensible only to the adults and the older children, it's clever to situate these very close to stage effects which will make at least part of the joke comprehensible to the very young.

> MOLOCH: I want to hear an owl cry and a church clock strike the hour. (*Instantly, distant bell chimes, and an owl shrieks nearby.*) Excellent.

The magic spells work on the victims like hypnotism and, as a trial, Bolligrew makes Blackheart dance in his clanking armour.

70

The Thwarting of Baron Bolligrew

It's also clever to introduce the dragon immediately after this spectacular scene. With the audience's appetite for stage effects sated, it's all the more effective to present the dragon just by switching on a pair of red eyes inside the blackness of a cave, while an amplified voice booms out. Bolt's moral preoccupations filter amusingly through even here: the dragon is interested in whether Oblong is a good man because good men have a distinctive flavour.

But before the bewitched Oblong can be fed to him, another obstacle is introduced. Back on the mainland, the Duke and his Knights are starting to feel schoolboyishly guilty about the dirty trick they've played on their old friend. So the Duke decides to visit the island in person and, travelling with one Knight, Sir Percival Smoothely-Smoothe, he starts on his journey just in time to make Moloch rack his evil brains for a new idea. How are they to proceed with their original plan and still send the Duke away satisfied? Moloch charges the Baron fifteen guineas for a solution to the new problem.

Preparations on the island for the Duke's visit are rather like preparations in a military camp for a high-ranking officer's inspection. Moloch's new idea is to make Oblong disgrace himself in front of the Duke. When he hears that he's never done anything disgraceful in his life, he orders the bewitched Knight-Errant to do all those things which for all those years he's restrained himself from doing. In other words, the effect of the magic is to release Oblong from his inhibitions, rather in the way that Pan released Jacko. Of course Oblong's behaviour is very different – and very funny. He greets the Duke as a 'backsliding old gormandizer', prodding his stomach and wondering out loud how many chocolate eclairs have gone in there. When the National Anthem is played, he dances a can-can, and snapping his fingers in the Duke's face, he utters the dreaded word 'knickers'.

It's then that we see why there are two magpies in the cast. By knocking Mazeppa over the head with a club, Mike is able to take his place and find out what spell Oblong is under. With Obidiah's help, he works the same spell on Bolligrew. Another neat point is made here: but for the magpie's thieving, which Oblong has tried to stop, they wouldn't have a prized possession of Bolligrew's at the hour of need. As it is, they can make use of the gold watch which, despite his promise, Mike has stolen and they order the Baron to confess how Oblong has been bewitched.

But even now Oblong's moral scruples work as an obstacle. Because the evidence against the Baron has been obtained through witchcraft, Oblong insists that it isn't legally valid. But everything can still be sorted out happily. Bolligrew helps Oblong to kill the dragon, who has now killed Moloch, though, being so wicked, he tasted disgusting. Finding that dragon-hunting is such good sport, the Baron decides to devote himself to it in the dragon-infested North and Oblong is made Baron of the islands.

The play ends with Oblong interrupting the story-teller and Mike interrupting him, as between them they give us a moral in verse:

> OBLONG : It's simply this: My dears, do-what-you-ought. When there's something you want, and you can't do without it. There are various ways of going about it —
>
> MAGPIE (*righteous*): And a very good way it is to – do – what – you – *should*.
>
> OBLONG : Exactly.
>
> MAGPIE : But a bit of what you fancy does yer good!
>
> OBLONG : Michael!
>
> MAGPIE : Awk!

SECOND INTERVIEW

R.H. *What I'd like to do, if you're agreeable, is take the plays separately and talk about your reactions to what I've written. But first of all, what's your general reaction to the whole thing?*

R.B. It's certainly the most immediate and penetrating comment on my work that I've had. My only criticism of your criticism is that you have perhaps missed how *carefully* I write. Just as there are sea and water images in *A Man for All Seasons,* there are mathematical puns in *Gentle Jack* – like the name of the Brackets, for instance. And I try to switch words with an Empsonian ambiguity. Or in that speech from *The Tiger and the Horse* which you quote on page 41, there is the image of the tiger though the word is never mentioned. Mrs Dean says 'I didn't know the answer then but I felt it get to its feet.' And then she goes on, 'The answer turned its head.' And then: 'Why must he be good just to listen to me? . . . And it came towards me.' 'Why does he never associate with me? Why have we never in anything been together?' And the answer. 'Sprang!' And at the beginning, in the early days of their marriage she 'felt' the answer – or tiger – so it is still inside her. Later it 'comes towards her,' so her tiger is now outside her, it has taken on a sort of independent existence from her, it's getting out of hand, and she is becoming irrational. I don't think audiences consciously notice this sort of thing but you are meant to feel the movement behind the speech like a tiger springing.

Yes, you do

I do think play-writing is more like poetry than prose because of these artificial tensions that the form imposes. One of the most comforting things that have ever been said to me was Peter Shaffer's remark after he'd seen *Gentle Jack* – 'But it's full of alexandrines.' He must have a good ear because the actors rightly didn't labour the rhythms.

Anything else in general before we take the plays individually?

That point you made off the cuff in the first interview rang a hell of a bell with me. About putting more of myself into the plays. I know you're right there.

Robert Bolt

Another thing that's struck me is the extent to which you change your style from play to play. It would be almost true to say that the six plays could have been written by six different men.

Yes. The one I was most at home in was *A Man for All Seasons*. Perhaps I should do more of that sort of thing. After all, Shakespeare never set plays in Jacobean London. Even in those days when even sewage regulations read like poetry, he felt it was a bit much to expect audiences to accept his people as their own contemporaries, and if he didn't attempt it then, who's going to get away with it now? Going back to a historical epoch gives you a kind of Dutch courage. You can make your characters theatrically big without embarrassment.

Of course, Beckett and Pinter have broken out of this. Their characters are abstracted out of circumstances. The questions 'What's his job? How much money is he earning?' are irrelevant to their characters, and the question of whether their behaviour is plausible simply doesn't arise.

What I was trying to do in *Gentle Jack* was to combine all the elements of ritual, dance and music in a specific modern context. And it didn't work. Sir Ralph Richardson said that a play is like a clock. You have to put it up there on the stage and stand away from it and either it goes or it doesn't. You can have the most beautifully complex mechanism which just doesn't go or you can have a cheap alarm clock of a play like *Charley's Aunt*. You can put that in a bucket of water and it still goes on ticking away. Or at the other extreme, *Hamlet*.

Or A Man for All Seasons

Thanks ... I feel a bit guilty about *A Man for All Seasons*.

Why?

Stylistically. I felt altogether that I was leaning too heavily on tradition. That the work being done by people like Pinter was to do with our day and age. Then there was The Theatre of Cruelty. And I couldn't make head or tail of it. I said to myself, I'm a young man and I'm living in the Sixties. My work ought to have more to do with what's happening now. David Lean gets very excited about the vapour trails that jets leave in the sky, but they leave me cold. I like sailing ships which have nothing really to do with today. I like very little modern architecture. I find it cheerless and forbidding, for the most

74

part, and I don't like much modern furniture. I like writing about good people; I don't like writing about villains. I'm more interested in behaviour than motive. The cliché has it that villains are more interesting, but that's not true, unless they're shot through with some kind of misgiving. I don't think I've written about any characters I totally dislike. Cromwell I have a good deal of sympathy for.

What about Pat in The Critic and the Heart?

Pat is everything I dislike in myself, I suppose.

Probably you'd prefer not to talk in too much detail about The Critic and the Heart *because I know you're in the process of rewriting it as* Brother and Sister.*

In the two speeches you quote of Pat's on page 22, I don't know whether this is convincing as the way a painter talks, but the intention is that at the end of the play, you still don't know whether he's a real painter or not.

Don't you? I had the impression you wanted us to think of him as really rather talented and this worried me because I felt from the way he talked that he wasn't.

We don't know. You never do *know* whether an artist is good or bad. Most competent judges thought that Van Gogh was just tragically self-deceived.

Surely, from the way a man talks about his work, you can usually form a pretty good idea of whether he's any good or not.

Perhaps you're right. But what *is* an artist? I have two definitions. All artists are liars in love with the truth. They have to be enthusiastic liars in order to invent freely. But they're not lying for gain. They want to embody a Truth. They have to do both. The really great thing of course is the man of action who's in love with the truth – Christ, Gandhi, Buddha. The second definition is similar: that they're all blackguards in love with virtue. I feel when I'm writing, that I'm sitting on Pandora's Box. If I let it open just that much, the lot will be out and away. Well that's a bit exaggerated, but something like that.

---

*One version of *Brother and Sister* was tried out at the Brighton Festival in 1967 with Dame Flora Robson, and another, in which William appears on stage, was tried out at the Bristol Old Vic in May 1968, with Sonia Dresdel. But Bolt wants to do more rewriting before the play comes to the West End.

Robert Bolt

Any other points on The Critic and the Heart?

This point about the amount of plot. I think all my plays except *A Man for All Seasons* have got too much plot in them. I get this feeling that I'm not giving audiences their money's worth. I find audiences impatient. There's nothing I like more than a bit of enjoyable argy-bargy but I have a conviction that the play should *develop* as it explains. This has been an abiding question for me. Audiences will take anything in the theatre, but they won't stand for a dead stop in the action. They make you pay for it. Not at the actual moment, but they start coughing three lines later.

One other point. In the speech you quote in page 20, I wouldn't agree that Winifred is romanticizing William. All this is literally true. *But she says she's never known anyone so gentle.*

He is gentle. He's also cruel. You must have known people like that. I don't know anyone who *isn't* like that, more or less.

So we get a sort of tie-up with the gentleness-cruelty theme in Gentle Jack

She's ambivalent about him of course. 'He *was* a villain . . . But he wasn't,' she says. Then in the next speech you quote on page 21, the idea is to show an unscrupulous man getting into a philosophical mood. One of the main questions in the whole relationship between Winifred and Reeves is whether she will be capable of reacting to his nasty way of using the letters. In *The Critic and the Heart* she isn't; in *Brother and Sister*, she is.

Shall we go on to Flowering Cherry?

Yes. You know, I don't agree with you that the characters are less interesting than in *The Critic and the Heart*. More ordinary, yes, but anyone who's pushed to crisis pitch is interesting. The fact of being an insurance salesman is neither here nor there.

No, his job doesn't matter, but if he's a dull man, can you make him interesting enough to carry the weight of a whole play? With a really dreary, commonplace little man, not likeable or in any way interesting, could you make him a satisfactory central character just because of a crisis in his life?

I think so, if I can show the crisis mounting in the right way.

Did you agree that Sir Ralph's performance was too big for Cherry?

I suppose so, if I'm to be honest, but he was so enchanting I was quite seduced by it.

There's certainly something about Cherry which is likeable – I mean in the script, quite apart from Sir Ralph.

But he doesn't do one likeable thing in the whole play.

No, but there's something about his appeals for sympathy in the scenes with Isobel which is hard to resist.

He's a child, a dreamer, that's why. Also the fact that the things he hates – life in the office and so on – are in fact hateful. I don't agree though with what you say on page 25 about the difficulty of believing that he'd stay for twenty years inside the office. Surely it's more difficult to imagine him being really rude to his office superiors, even once. Isn't it obvious from that speech about walking on corpses that he's a man who substitutes violent words for action? Like the Flowering Cherry – another pun – you know, that tree that's grown in the suburbs. It puts out clouds of pink blossom, but nothing happens. No fruit.

I quoted that speech about walking on corpses because it shows he's capable of saying quite good things. He must have quite a good mind.

Yes he's half educated and he's read quite a lot and he has imagination and memory, but no courage. I'm half-way through a film script for David Lean on Gandhi and what emerges mainly from the work is that Gandhi had superlative courage. Whatever occurred to him as right he just did without fear.

The point I didn't succeed in making in the play was that in the end, I found a failure on Isobel's part too. She was unable to understand that what he wanted was the dream. When it comes out that he doesn't really want an actual orchard, she calls it a lie. In other words, she really wishes he were a different kind of man. It's a story of a man who was inadequate, which is a universal condition.

There was a story about a surgeon who didn't live a very virtuous life and when his friends asked him, 'What are you going to say when you're called to the Bar of Heaven?' his answer was, 'Oh I think I shall be all right. I'm going to take the skeleton of a small child who died of spinal meningitis and demand an explanation.' Well, I shall take Cherry with me and say 'He was inadequate and knew he was inadequate and didn't like it, but what the hell did you expect him to do about it?'

77

Robert Bolt

So Isobel is as much of a fantasist as he is in expecting him to be able to opt for the orchard?

A more culpable fantasist in that respect. This is what's meant to be shown by the fact that Cherry doesn't even toy with the idea of the orchard when she presents it to him as realizable. But when he immediately baulked at it, the audience started laughing at him and their sympathy went to her. And of course cowardice is funny. But fear isn't. And he is simply terrified.

What about the other characters?

You're right about Judy. More should have been made of her. She should perhaps have been the key.

Anything else you disagree with?

When Cherry gives advice to Tom, telling him that it's no fun in bed unless you have respect for your partner, it has a bearing on Isobel. She has no respect for him. And the speech of hers you quote on page 28 is *meant* to be a string of clichés.

What does she feel while she's talking?

She's just trying to keep the family together. Which is what she always does. I know how I'd end the play now. With him making an awful noise, and her coming back – she can't leave him – and saying, 'For goodness sake stop making that awful noise. They can hear you at the end of the road.' That's the actual end of that situation. People just peg on, for the most part, I'm afraid.

Now let's go on to The Tiger and the Horse.

Of course you're right to say that it isn't a play about the bomb, but you can't write a play that even mentions the bomb because the thing itself is so enormous that it's like hanging a cannon ball on a Christmas tree: the whole thing just topples over. Every time the bomb is mentioned, everything else becomes ghostlike. What you say in the middle of page 33 is very perspicacious but I think you've partly missed the point of the pun about the horse. When Slate talks about Mrs Dean's father who subsisted almost entirely upon oats, Dean says, 'I'm reputed to resemble him.' I'm almost ashamed to mention it but oats are what horses live on. And on pgae 35 you say the question of whether Dean is justified in pleading ignorance of the diplomatic and military considerations is only touched in passing. Surely it's clear that I don't approve? I mean very few people have full knowledge of those considerations, but everyone is responsible none the less.

The point about Dean is that he's a man who'd do anything rather than have his wife hurt. What I was trying to say – and I know this didn't come out clearly – is that someone who is really engaged with another human being will find willy-nilly that he is interested in the bomb. Not that he ought to be, but *is*. Only if he is *totally* selfish, can he not be. But someone should have said it. I had at this time such a belief in the power of symbols. As in that poem of George Herbert's, *Easter Wings*, where the words are printed in the shape of two butterflies; Herbert must have thought that this would help. It doesn't. But I wouldn't have said that Dean had made any moral compromises just for the sake of climbing the academic ladder. His motives are bigger. He's a good man who has ignored the trouble at home as he contemplated infinite spaces. You know: 'The eternal silence of these infinite spaces terrifies me.'

But when he holds out the pen for Gwendoline to sign the petition, what's he thinking? Is Stella right when she says that he knew this would have the effect of making her mother refuse to sign or is Gwendoline right when she says he wanted her to sign?

That's interesting. He's in a bad temper of course. I think he wanted her to sign and have done with it. 'To hell with it – I'm not going to be put in this position.' Pessimists are often preoccupied by their stance.

Then on page 36, Slate's speech, which you quote as light relief, isn't entirely light relief. There's a tie-up between his account of space and Dean's, which comes at the end of the act, and the mention of a tea-cosy refers forwards to the one which Gwendoline will later wear. Although the whole speech is mocking, the experience has obviously excited him and there's a hint of relativity, and a hint of madness, when he talks about the gentle shaking motion, well calculated to *unhinge*, and of 'falling upwards'. So, in a way, the speech anticipates everything that Dean has seen up there in the stars.

Then page 39, it isn't just the cocky lover who is deflated, it's also the opinionated politician. When the real child is there, everything is very different.

Yes, that's true. Any other points?

Robert Bolt

In Mrs Dean's big speech at the end, when she says, 'He sleeps like an angel! Like a pig!' the point is that angels and pigs sleep in much the same way, for much the same reason. Human beings sleep less well.

Then, at the very end of the play, the point about taking the telescope is that he's going to take another look at the universe to see whether he can see anything more there. I hope he did, but doubt it. He's found out that love is the only thing which can rescue people from isolation. This I got from Buber, who says that when you become really deeply involved with another person, you open yourself and God slips in.

That's very good, and it brings us rather aptly to A Man for All Seasons.

What I feel about *A Man for All Seasons* is that it's a bit of a prevarication. Or say it was a farewell salute to traditional values, taken *tout court*. I like them, as I like antique furniture, and I feel at home with them, but they don't happen to be mine, not *tout court*, so I've no right to them. Also, a historical character isn't open-ended, like a contemporary, which is an artistic ace card to have in your hand; but each member of the audience is open-ended. You can never fully know a man till he's dead.

The only point of yours that I'd really want to question is the statement that More's preoccupation with selfhood was anachronistic. At least it's a point of Anthony Kenny's but you make it your own. I would have said that this business of trying to draw an outline around yourself was very much a Renaissance concept. To thine own self be true. Raleigh and Marlowe were both flirting very seriously with atheism – Faustus makes experiments in trying to find himself. And selfhood becomes a preoccupation with Lear and Hamlet. It was no longer a matter of just keeping your nose clean. The question is 'Who the hell am I?' *Macbeth* is a play about the chaos which overtakes a man when he loses touch with himself. There's a sense of precariousness overtaking the medieval world order which defined a man from outside.

But none of these examples you've quoted are Christian. The speech of More's that worries me most is the one I quoted on page 44. 'What matters to me is not whether it's true or not but that I believe it to be true, or rather not that I believe it, but that I believe it.'

He was being splenetic there. The others were pressuring him and it was something like a fit of temper. The key speech is the speech about angels, which you quote on page 51. This is All My Own Work, since you raise the point – there's no quotation in it. And I think any intelligent Christian in his day would have equated soul with self. *Doesn't the self die?*

The soul is the informing intelligence. This part of the self subsists after death and is rejoined with its sphere of matter at the Bodily Resurrection. I think. I'm not a theologian.

But if More believed in the individual conscience as an arbiter – if it's right to do what you yourself believe is right – what about the question of inconsistency in condemning Roper's heresy?

He was narrow-minded (that is, by modern standards) about certain things and any man is sensitive about his son-in-law. But if Roper had offered to become a Catholic just to please him, he would have said to Margaret, 'You will *never* marry that man.' And according to Chambers, he was outlandishly tolerant and humane as Chancellor. 'I have no window to look into another man's soul.' There's no evidence that he ever had anyone prosecuted for religious belief or religious practice. I believe in freedom of conscience. So do you. But I wouldn't tolerate killing Jews, even in a man who thought it morally right. Or this is inconsistent. What's amazing about More is the perfection of his behaviour both in detail and overall. A nearly faultless performance, but without any recourse to a transcendental explanation. And his style was so good. He was a perfect gentleman – a breathtaking performance as a human being. He knocked off *Utopia*, cleaned up the law courts, ran this house where he entertained all the celebrities of his day, kept up his friendships with noblemen and people like Colet and Erasmus and behaved like John Bunyan. This is why people like the play. They think 'Thank Christ, somebody can do it. I may not be able to, but life *can* be that perfect.' And he didn't do anything that you or I couldn't have done. St Francis talked to the birds, but anyone at his best could do what More did. He had taste, wit, courtesy, consideration – he was marvellously witty: 'In Utopia,' he wrote, 'the priests are of exceeding holiness, and therefore very few.'

Alice was the only one who defeated him, the only one to whom he

Robert Bolt

made just a naked appeal – 'Don't do this to me' – because she was a
primitive. Very primitive apparently. But he made all his guests
treat her respectfully.

*Is there any historical justification for placing such emphasis on his
family life?*

Oh yes, it was famous. And tremendously important to him. He loved
his home. That's my only criticism of Paul Scofield's interpretation.
He has such presence as an actor that the moment he came on,
you knew this was something special. It shouldn't have been, not
then – just a man in his home. But you do also see More in col-
lision with quite a number of different factions and interests outside
home.

*I feel though that the social context could have helped you more in your
picture of the individual. As in a painting.*

Possibly, but my individualism, as you call it, isn't a reaction against
Marxism. On the contrary, it's a mild development of it. The Marxist
social analysis is a questionable one. Many followers of Marx have
become more royalist than the King and Marx himself was a product
of nineteenth-century materialism. The Marxists have fallen into their
own trap and accepted the alienation of the worker. They talk about a
classless society but people suffer individually – they're born that way,
they live that way and they die that way.

I accept what you say about the form of work and religion being
conditioned by society, but the experience of work and religion is
irretrievably an individual one. Wolves hunt in packs and that dictates
the form of the hunt, but they feel the sheep's flesh in their jaws
individually.

*But it isn't just a matter of form. Hunting isn't the same thing as
working.*

Oh yes it is.

*But don't you think it could have helped the personal foreground if you'd
been more interested in the way people worked in the sixteenth century?*

It's true that the groundswell of historical popular opinion isn't
there. The Common Man starts off as Adam, in tights, and he says,
'If they'd let me come on naked, I could have shown you something
of my own.' And a lot of his speeches end up with the word 'common'
or have it in them towards the end. 'That's only Common Sense' or

'It's common' when More asks after his wife and he says she's losing her shape. It means 'shape' as 'identity'. The whole play is a sustained pun. But yes, the Common Man is less and more than sixteenth-century opinion.

The real confrontation between More and the Common Man comes when More says he'll miss him and this makes him hopping mad. He'd have much preferred it if More had condemned him. He's lost his self; he's become just a shifting commodity. But that shows the danger of being a good man: his mere presence is a standing reproach, if he won't say yes. It's not enough that he doesn't say no. Henry, Richard Rich, Wolsey, Cromwell, Norfolk, they all love More – and they kill him.

Incidentally there is some historical justification for the character of Rich. More knew him as a young man and helped him. He adored More and wanted to be employed by him.

The relationship works very well. The trouble – and I know this is inevitable in a play – is that you can't show the life of the mind.

That's true, but I wasn't just taking More as an excuse for writing a play about the self. I think increasingly that behaviour is more interesting than motive. That's why I wrote *Lawrence of Arabia* the way I did. What he did is more interesting than whatever the explanation is. Shall we go on to your points about *Gentle Jack* now?

Fine.

There's a deliberate send-up of the psychiatrist in the way Pan speaks – or rather of the *Reader's Digest – Esquire* Magazine concept of the psychiatrist. There's also some deliberate camp in Pan's part. Pan is neither nice nor nasty – he is, as his name implies, everything. It's a pessimistic play and what I was trying to say in it was that life was unsatisfactory either with or without Pan. I think it's a phrase of G. K. Chesterton's that a dog can never fail as a dog, but a human being can very easily fail as a human being. How much free play are you to allow to the side of the personality that is a madman and an infant? The few critics who chanced their arm on the play either said it was too obvious or too obscure. There was one who thought it meant that a little of what you fancy does you good. I was trying to say that the whole of what you fancy includes murder. I was trying to make a Pan who was simultaneously squalid and magnificent – which

83

is what Nature is. You can't have the whole of the one without the other, but we try. That's what civilization is about.

Morgan is the antithesis of Pan. He's taken it for granted that natural life is unsatisfactory. And thinks it childish to persuade yourself that it can be otherwise. Pan says 'Take a tiger'. But for Morgan, nothing means anything except figures, to which everything is finally reducible by Science. I think the idea behind the play is that we tend today to carry around a basketful of completely irreconcilable philosophies – Marxism, Freudianism, Taoism, scientific detachment – which never get amalgamated into any one view of life. People hop from one to the other according to convenience. The play's being in two halves was deliberate. I wanted to show man straddling the two positions. But I know this failed, as you say, because the audience didn't get it.

Now, your point on page 45 about the rustic workers' lacking three-dimensionality. They are really a chorus, a kind of joint Common Man. They too carry out stage directions. It's a pity you didn't say more about Greeves, the kind of Marxist one. He's an interesting character because he accepts all our premises, but draws the opposite conclusions.

Did you ever, at any stage of planning, intend to make Violet more important in the action?

No. Why?

I thought the opening scene in the office conveyed some kind of promise that you'd go on to explore her more fully and exploit the glamour that there always is in great power.

I think millions of pounds are always exciting. And the audience loved the business of looking at the cards, deciding what to buy and what to sell, taking up the option to buy Egyptian Metals and planning to go on buying till Iranian Silver became less healthy or whatever it was. Again, this is intended to be a ritual of finance, not the way finance is conducted.

But there's a difference, isn't there, between the rituals that contain the life of a thing and others which miss it?

Yes it becomes too abstract, perhaps, diagrammatic. Violet was order and authority, you see. Which are the same thing, unhappily. She felt guilty about the old man, Jacko's father, not because of his death, but because he was a *man*, and she ought not to have won. He was probably the only man she ever met of whom she felt that.

The imagery in the speech you quote on page 57 is intended as a bombardment – 'mists and muck, hard horn, wet orifice, the skyline and the greasy pail, dung, hung game, cattle giving birth and being killed, the workers and their wives, sharp knives, stags, stallions . . .' Pan would say 'You've taken absolutely everything there that's delightful.' But Jacko wants to get away from the sexual and physical. He wants to become like Violet, which is why he's gone to the office. *Yes I think I know why this speech doesn't succeed for me. The imagery is so rich and the depth of depression is so great that it ought to work poetically, almost like one of Hamlet's soliloquies. But it doesn't – I think for two reasons. One is that the images don't grow together organically and the other is that after the squeaking boots and the papers dropped all over the office floor, we can't take Jacko all that seriously. You establish him as a figure of fun and you even draw on theatrical or vaudeville conventions. It's almost like Laurel and Hardy.*

He's a nit, a clown.

Why did you make him so clumsy, such a fumbler?

Because a man who has totally turned his back on spontaneity is bound to be a fool. But he's honest. He says what he hates about Nature. Until the country scenes, he's all City and it just makes an idiot of him.

Don't you think you need a hero that the audience can identify with more?

You're right. First he's abnormally inhibited and then abnormally uninhibited. He's only normal in the scene with Penelope. It's all too much like a diagram. Gaston is deliberately like the cliché idea of a Frenchman: he's the man who's got a tame Pan. Which is why the girl says he looks as though he's got his clothes on when he's naked. Mrs Treadgold is the only one who's free of all this. She's an innocent. At one point in the play she falls when Jacko frightens her, and suddenly his pity is aroused – and that's a turning point.

In the speech on pages 61–2 which you say is difficult, what Pan is saying is that there's nothing to be afraid of. Man is split because he's frightened, but of himself, not of anything else. Then at the end I try to turn the tables. What I'm trying to do is make a real Pan. We are so far gone in sentimentality that what people think of is

Robert Bolt

Puck of Pook's Hill. But Pan is a madman. He produces honeysuckle and daisies in one hand and the bubonic plague in the other. It's all one to him.

This is fine, but it seems to me that the changes in his mode of speaking aren't entirely controlled or focused.

Maybe not. But at least they are deliberate. The other thing about Pan is that he's pathetic. He's having a hard time of it now. When he appeals to the audience for a natural man, someone who will stand up for what he *wants,* he's like someone trying to cadge a sixpence. No one believes in him these days though he's much talked about. But I don't think he misled Jacko about the bargain. He offered himself on loan. Jacko borrows him and then it turns out that he only wants part, not the whole of the loan.

But when they actually strike the bargain, he says it's free of interest and absolutely without obligation. This gives the impression that Jacko can just take what he wants for as long as he wants, so long as he stays out of doors. I don't think anyone can be expected to understand from what Jack says that Jacko may be under some obligation to kill, if he doesn't want to.

That was meant to be my attack on easy-going Freudianism – the feeling that you can just take what you want from Pan and that it will do you good, like a holiday. But I don't entirely understand the audience reaction. I don't know why Kenneth Williams didn't get a laugh on 'Is there an animal in the house?'

Could it have been because they were too frightened about the killing that was coming up?

I was rather depending on the Brechtian stylization to keep them from getting too involved.

But surely it needs involvement here. Doesn't the play rather suffer from this all through? You give the impression of thinking you can have it both ways at the same time – that you can draw them in and push them back simultaneously.

Yes, that's quite right. And I didn't get away with it, did I? . . . I do think though that you might have commented on the rhythms a little more. In the speech you quote at the top of page 65 for, instance, I think the rhythms are quite good.

Finally, there's a distinction at the end of the play between killing and murder. Of course Pan can kill for himself. He's killing millions all the time. He only kills Morgan in order to get the chorus to murder Jacko. At the end of it he shouts 'Murder' and he's gone. I think that's all on *Gentle Jack*. My crippled child, the one I'm specially defensive about.

So we come to Baron Bolligrew.

Children are marvellous to write for. They were on to it straight away that Oblong's motives weren't pure in going to the Bolligrew Islands – that his vanity was flattered by the robe. And that later Moloch was playing on his moral vanity to get possession of it. Children see what's there, neither more nor less.

Because they haven't got into habits.

Yes. It's interesting that the children you took were bothered when the story-teller spoke to the characters.

Other children weren't?

No, the only thing they resented was one 'Now children' which was only put in to send up the adults who talk like that, but they thought they were being patronized.

My own favourite scene is the corruption of Blackheart by Bolligrew, when he convinces him that he should challenge Oblong to a duel.

You were in the play yourself in the first production, weren't you?

Just for fun, I was the dragon – my voice coming out of the cave. It was hard to get the cast to act the play for the reality and leave the nonsense to take care of itself, but it works much better that way. I've never had a perfectly satisfactory Moloch. He's intended to be an awful old don with a terrible contempt for Bolligrew and Blackheart and a huge relish for money, not a mad magician.

In the scene with the Duke and the Knights in Act Two, it's not just that they're guilty about Oblong, they're also bored. There are rumours about a dragon in Little Gidding and a damsel in distress in East Coker, but these are just rumours and there's nothing to do. It's the boredom of wrongdoing. There's that marvellous remark of Conrad's that most of the good and most of the evil that gets done is done because people get bored with doing either the one or the other.

One point you didn't comment on – realizing that it's his moral vanity that has let him down, Oblong vows never to carry sword again. Then the dragon roars and immediately he seizes his sword. Similarly, he wants to have no truck with trickery – to keep his means as pure as his ends – but he has to rely on the morally deplorable Magpie at the crisis. I like this business of letting the action contradict the word. Children get it quickly because they see as well as listen. Of all the plays I've written, this is the one that's given me the most pleasure.